A Taste for Adventure

By the same author

WHERE THE TRAILS RUN OUT

IN THE STEPS OF STANLEY

A Taste for Adventure

John Blashford-Snell

Best wishes

HUTCHINSON OF LONDON

Hutchinson & Co. (Publishers) Ltd
3 Fitzroy Square, London W1P 6JD

London Melbourne Sydney Auckland
Wellington Johannesburg and agencies
throughout the world

First published 1978

Set in Monotype Garamond

Printed in Great Britain by The Anchor Press Ltd
and bound by Wm Brendon & Son Ltd
both of Tiptree, Essex

British Library CIP data

Blashford-Snell, John Nicholas
A taste for adventure.
1. Blashford-Snell, John Nicholas
2. Explorers – Biography
I. Title
910'.92'4 G246.B55

ISBN 0 09 136010 2

This book is dedicated to the memory of three men whom I greatly admired and respected:

'Bish' – my father,
Brigadier Jack Fletcher
and
Major Johnnie Braddell-Smith

They were all courageous, with a taste for adventure, a healthy contempt for difficulties and dangers, and a spirit that lives forever.

Contents

Illustrations

IN THE TEXT

Acknowledgements

In this sequel to *Where the Trails Run Out* I have again tried not to write an autobiography, but more a collection of experiences involving my friends in many lands. I owe a great deal to those mentioned here and much to many whose names do not appear. If any credit is due, it is to them. I repeat what I have said in the previous work: that I count myself fortunate to have such an understanding and helpful circle of friends, and privileged to have led some of the finest people – servicemen and civilians – in the world.

I am again most grateful to Mr H. M. Stephen, managing director of the *Daily Telegraph*, for his continued advice and encouragement, and to the Rt Hon William Deedes, editor of the *Daily Telegraph*, for his kind permission to publish the photographs taken by Kenneth Mason. I am also extremely grateful to Christopher Sainsbury for allowing me to use his photographs. My appreciative thanks go to the editor of the *Daily Express*, Mr Derek Jameson, for his kind permission to use the cartoon by Giles, and also to Mr John Edwards, editor of the *Yorkshire Post* for his co-operation and support.

My thanks also go to John Prebble and Messrs Secker and Warburg, publishers of his book, *The Darien Disaster* (1968), for kindly allowing me to quote from this valuable work, which did so much to help us trace the former Scots colony in Panama.

I am also deeply indebted to Betty Starling and my long-suffering wife Judith, who have done so much of the typing and proof-reading, and to Frances Chidell for her literary advice.

Two soldiers have contributed to the book: Lance Corporal Pascoe, who helped with the maps, and Corporal Thomas, my driver, who kept the staff car at a steady pace on so many long journeys, allowing me to write as we drove.

My most sincere gratitude goes to the British Army and in particular to my regiment, the Royal Engineers, who have always given so much encouragement and support to one of their madder sappers!

1. A way of life

Adjusting my *shemagh*, I raised the cine-camera to my eye; through the view-finder zoomed up the column of swaying, sand-coloured trucks, winding their way slowly up the *jebel* track. The camera motor purred gently, recording all for posterity. 'Thump–crump', went the artillery, and the distant roar of the ever watchful jets was a constant reminder that in this vacant Arabian landscape, we were at war.

Continuing to film, I brought the telephoto lens to bear on a leading three-tonner that was nearing the head of the valley. Suddenly it reared up in an eruption of dust, out of which a body hurtled skyward. 'Purr', went the camera, 'Ba–bam', came the blast wave that shook us. Staff Sergeant Lightowler, driving our truck, muttered an oath.

'The gunners have had a bloody drop short,' yelled the lance corporal on the machine-gun behind me.

But through the long lens I had seen it all too clearly.

'No, it's a mine,' I replied. 'Probably a Russian anti-tank.'

The column had halted, no one moved; eyes scanned the parched earth for the hidden death-traps and the hilltops for the expected ambush. The silence was short-lived. Diving steeply from the sun, the Strike-masters screamed in to protect the column as the dust and smoke cleared from around the stricken vehicle.

'Holdfast,* this is Sunray,'† came Brigadier Jack Fletcher's voice on the radio. 'Looks like a job for you.'

'Wilco,' I replied, jumping down on to the desert floor. The sappers needed little bidding; already they were assembling mine detectors, prodders and rolls of white marking tape. Walking cautiously along the tyre tracks, we were soon beside the unlucky truck. The right front wheel had disappeared and the vehicle lay nose-down in the crater. Three wounded men

* Army radio terminology for engineers.

† Army radio terminology for a commander.

sprawled in the merciless sun, their crimson blood oozing into the powdery soil. The air was heavy with the smell of high explosive. The mine had been laid at just the right spot in a defile and had got the mortar platoon of the Muscat Regiment, the third vehicle in the column. Somehow Patrick Brook's Saladin armoured cars and my own leading engineer section's truck had passed over it unscathed.

Now, as the sappers worked outward from the crater, clearing the ground and marking the safe area, there came the 'Whacka–whacka–whacka' of an approaching Huey helicopter. Green smoke swirled up to give the wind direction as the Omani medical orderlies lifted those with shattered limbs on to stretchers. The casualty evacuation took only a few moments and then the Huey was hurtling back to Salalah, where Mary, our brigadier's wife, would nurse them at the base hospital.

Now the track was clear and I could see the lean, tanned figure of Staff Sergeant Lightowler signalling forward 'Mammoth' and 'Mastadon', our clanking, semi-armoured bulldozers, to winch the smashed vehicle out of the crater and into a position where the recovery vehicle could hoist it up into a suspended tow. Patrick Brook was in his turret, scanning the shimmering horizon through binoculars. As I climbed up on the armoured car beside him he smiled and the dust fell from his begrimed features.

'We're all set to advance again,' I said.

'Let's hope we don't get another,' he replied. 'The Adoo are lying pretty low and may have something up their sleeves.' Then, looking thoughtful, he added, 'What happens if Mammoth or Mastadon get hit? We've nothing to tow those monsters.'

'Either I'll blow them to bits or fit up a fiendish booby-trap to prevent pilfering and we'll have an interesting little recovery operation when the war's moved on,' I remarked.

'You're a menace,' laughed the man who had shared my bottle of scotch in the Persian Forward Position the previous night.

'On to White City,' we cheered and the Dhofar Brigade lurched forward again.

We ploughed on through the choking dust, engines roaring, *shemaghs* fluttering, radios cackling, guns thumping and the jets whining overhead. I turned to my radio operator.

'Enjoying yourself?'

'Aye – this is right adventurous living,' yelled the Yorkshire lad above the din.

'That just about sums it up,' I thought. 'My whole way of life.'

I could clearly remember the day when Father, a war-like Army padre, had returned from France in 1944 to disperse the rooks that were blocking the church gutters. This he had done with a rifle, to the detriment of the roof. My mother was also an exciting person. She adored animals and had kept a wild boar as a pet in New Zealand; twenty-eight cats, three dogs, a horse and a couple of foxes shared the Herefordshire vicarage where I grew up. One Christmas Day the master of fox hounds called in for a port after church. He was a big, hearty man and had just emptied his second glass when he caught sight of the vixen asleep on the fireside mat. His monocle dropped from his eye.

'Oh my God, Vicar,' he groaned, 'the end is nigh, must be DTs at last.'

My parents looked up in surprise, but the MFH was already on his way out, muttering, 'Never thought it would come to this – bloody foxes everywhere.' He was gone before Mother could explain.

Brutus was a huge, stupid Saint Bernard, who roared rather than barked and would leap on to the garage roof to pull down my drying rabbit skins. He always won the fancy dress contest at the Church dog show and was a passable, if clumsy, gun dog. Unfortunately he couldn't tell the difference between rabbits, cats or small dogs and, one day, ate a poor, deaf old pekingese in the act of cocking its leg on the war memorial. I tried to comfort the grief-stricken owner by pointing out that the end had been both quick and painless and, anyway, the peke had had a good innings. Furthermore, I mentioned that my eleven-stone friend, who now sat beside me looking utterly dejected and dribbling with dismay, felt strongly about dogs of oriental origin desecrating a British war memorial. My reasoning was not appreciated.

Much of my childhood was spent in the company of this massive animal. He was at his worst in cars, slobbering abominably and frequently being sick, usually all over my grandmother and her cat. However, the good lady was of solid Jersey stock and, having been married to a John Blashford-Snell, had buried him and wed another, now deceased, before

I knew her. Even a vomiting Saint Bernard did not deter Granny, who kept her false teeth in weak brandy at night and accompanied us on many wartime journeys in Britain, when we travelled in the wake of the 53rd Welsh Division in which Father was a chaplain. She also had a parrot. It was green and it swore, belched and bit. In short, it was a revolting bird which annoyed both my canine friend and my godmother, Aunt Jess.

Jessica Le Brun was quite a girl. Her medals told of proficiency as a nursing sister with the French Red Cross in World War I and her photograph album showed numerous handsome young men who had pursued her whilst she tore around Jersey in her AC sports car. Now, World War II had cut her off from her beloved island and she spent her time sticking pins into an image of Hitler and, in her spare moments, filled bombs with TNT in an armaments factory.

My mother's family was English and my grandfather, George Sadler, was a big, amusing man. Living the life of a country gentleman in a Suffolk village, he had engaged Zeppelins with his sporting rifle from the roof of the Hall in 1918, captured an escaped circus python with the tractor, almost killed the local vicar with a trick truncheon and collected a runaway bull on the bonnet of his Armstrong-Sidley. His local hairdresser, on a rare visit to London, was amazed to be stared at by people whom he heard mutter, 'That's Barber Rowe from Braintree.' Convinced he was famous, the poor man was sadly shaken when he eventually discovered that George had pinned a notice on his back, which read, 'Barber Rowe from Braintree'.

Although I greatly admired George, I knew my godparents rather better. Lord and Lady Forester had travelled widely and it was their stories of big-game hunting and adventure that really made me long for a life of excitement.

My godfather was a soldier and had commanded the Royal Horse Guards. I often asked him where the German Maxim gun that was mounted at Willey Hall had come from, but he always smiled and just said, 'Something my regiment picked up in the Great War.' It was not until after he had died that I learned he had captured it single-handed. He had lived a wonderful life in the days of the Empire, hitch-hiking from Cape to Cairo, exploring the upper reaches of the Congo and, above all, devoting himself to the service of others. His particular love was Shropshire where he spent many years helping people and following his hobby as a naturalist and a sportsman. He lived out most of his final years in the other land he loved – Africa – and finally died peacefully in Rhodesia in 1977. The patience and understanding this kindly man showed me as a small scruffy schoolboy were to be a lasting inspiration.

I was also most fortunate to have a super aunt and uncle who lived in a cottage they had largely built themselves in the Welsh mountains. In those wild hills I could stalk rabbits with an air-rifle, watch tumbling miniature versions of the Victoria Falls and explore worked-out lead mines.

In the more sophisticated south, I had other relatives with vintage sports cars and a flare for practical engineering.

My 'Just William' existence progressed through 'prep', a choir school in sleepy Worcestershire, where my voice had broken early, and where I learned poker in the commoners' stalls. At home for holidays, my musical enjoyment was confined to playing a drum, which made Brutus howl; a ghastly and unsociable noise. So I turned my attention to the church organ; alas, the organist was unsympathetic and, in a mood of sullen revenge, I took a rat that Granny's ginger cat had been gnawing in the wood shed and popped it down one of the organ pipes. With evil glee, I sat in the choir stalls next day, awaiting the awful noise that would result from the rodent rattling on the reed. However, it was not to be. True, there was a strange sound; then, oh horror, the rat flew out and landed on a choir girl's lap. 'Eekkk,' screamed the maiden and, unseen, I seized the creature and secreted it in my hassock. They all scolded the poor girl; no one believed her and I consoled myself with the thought that the rat had lived to be played another day.

My father, believing that I was a useless waster, encouraged me to do something positive to help at home. Therefore, with reluctance, I agreed to rise before dawn on Wednesdays and ring the church bell for mid-week early communion. The searing cold in the unheated rectory bit through me like an arctic wind, as I stumbled through the snow to open the heavy vestry door and tugged at the aged bell-rope. Even an illicit nip of Father's brandy did little to fortify me and I knew that if I were to survive, I must find a better solution.

It came to me like a vision – indeed it may have been divine providence that showed me the way. The great bell was within view of my window and I quickly discovered that a round of

.300 rook rifle would produce a ring to waken the dead. Twenty shots and we had filled five pews, but alas, the resultant ricochets may have had more to do with it. As the last of the faithful scampered into the cover of the church porch, Father, in a biblical rage, reminded me that it was a house of peace. Nevertheless, he realized that we must move forward with the times and thus, by my next holidays, a gramophone and loud-speaker system had been installed to give a rendering of a slightly tinny version of 'Bow Bells' and other well-known peals. Not only did this increase Father's congregation, but when I turned the volume up to full power we even pulled in a few of the rival vicar's flock. Whilst fellow clerics muttered in the cathedral cloisters about progressive parsons, Pa enjoyed a full house.

In my new role as keeper of the records, I was responsible for this device. But, by now, I had grown older and had become friendly with the milkman's dark-eyed daughter, who sang in our choir. This temptress dared me to put a certain disc on the machine. Was ever Adam led astray by Eve? Thus, one day the parishioners were greeted with a jolly ballad, 'Captain Brown, Captain Brown, he played his ukelele as the ship went down'. In a final defiant gesture, I switched it on full volume to the deaf aid system for the last few bars, which sent the rows of pensioners bouncing from their seats.

It was perhaps understandable that my parents should encourage me to attend a school as far away from home as possible. Thus, in 1950, I arrived at Victoria College, Jersey. Granite-built, it stood fortress-like above St Helier. In the high-windowed classrooms, generations of Channel Islanders, including my father, had studied hard to gain places in the establishments of the Empire and, also, for the chosen few, a venerated position in the dignified local government, the States.

In my spare time, I continued a scouting career in the school troop and rose rapidly to the rank of patrol leader. The Wolf Patrol, a strangely apt name for my group, were excellent air-gun shots, firelighters and trackers. However, a camp in Rozel woods with some enterprising Girl Guides did not altogether please our scout master, who gave us an afternoon's lecture on the facts of life and the sins of the flesh (although the milkman's daughter had beaten him to it!).

At this point I decided that if I were going to be licentious,

I might as well do it properly, so I joined the school cadet corps. As cadets go, we were a pretty good unit. Our commander, Colonel Bill Eden, a firm but fair disciplinarian, had a flair for getting the best out of youngsters. He was also extremely keen on rifle shooting, which, being a major sport in Jersey, played an important part in our training. The island was full of retired officers who regularly shot alongside us in local matches. One eccentric major did much to encourage us and was also a source of amusement, especially when the aged spaniel, which always crouched beside him on the firing point, would break wind just as his master's watery, blood-shot eye had found the aiming mark and as he was in the very act of squeezing the trigger. The resultant shot would go wide of the target and, in a terrible rage, the major would boot the offensive animal off the point.

The occupation of the Channel Islands by the Germans in World War II was clearly evident: formidable concrete bunkers littered the cliffs, and the narrow valleys were a mass of tunnels. Guns, mines and all the paraphernalia of war were easily obtainable by adventurous schoolboys and how we survived was a miracle. Lugers were bought and sold in the changing rooms, Spandau machine-guns were stripped and cleaned in attics, whilst chemistry classes were essential for the understanding of bombs and explosives. At weekends we would cycle to remote areas to test our illegal toys. The absence of a paid police force in country districts greatly facilitated our pastime. Sadly there were accidents, some fatal, some almost fatal and others, simply hair-raising. As our knowledge of chemistry progressed, we learnt to make nitro-glycerine and, with this, blew open sealed bunkers in the search for more weapons and ammunition. Most of the nitro was made in a friend's greenhouse, because we believed that if it exploded we'd be better off inside, as presumably the glass would fly outwards!

In an effort to turn our minds to more peaceful topics, our headmaster, Colonel Ronnie Postill, created a compulsory debating society. Thus, all sixth-formers had to learn to speak in public, a valuable training that has stood many an old Victorian in good stead. To liven up our debates, a mock election was held. At once an evil bunch of us formed the 'Neo-Fascist' party. 'Nellie' Le Geyt became poet laureate and composed party political ballads, whilst Adrian Troy, Bungle Colson and

John Gwyther became henchmen to myself as 'Blashford Von Schnell', the dictator. The population of Jersey was more than mildy surprised to see our Nazi uniforms, armbands and steel helmets. However, it was not until our storm-troopers raised a fourteen-foot German banner over the school that our patient headmaster intervened. Nevertheless, for weeks the election campaign raged with its incredible dramas and satire; mainly centred on the controversial problem of the emancipation of the mole. Mass meetings were held and hecklers dragged off screaming by my black-shirts to the showers, where they were treated to a cold wash-down fully clothed! Party songs were sung at midnight sessions in a secret beer cellar. It was all great fun and to everyone's horror, we almost won the final election.

Incredibly, I managed to pass my exam for Sandhurst and continued to spend much of my school holidays with the Territorial Army. Father was chaplain of a Monmouthshire gunner regiment and thus I learnt the intricacies of anti-aircraft defence. Most members of our unit had seen service in the war and regarded their training camps as holidays. Regular officers, who had the misfortune to be posted to the various gunnery stations we visited, lived in dread of our arrival.

Of course there were great occasions when the regiment excelled itself. One such day was the visit of the Lord Lieutenant. By the time he arrived, monocle in eye, thrashing his breeches with his riding crop and muttering, 'Ypres, the Somme and Haig', our guns were already in action. With deafening noise, twenty-four 3.7s hurled tons of high explosive skyward at a red canvas sleeve being towed some 1000 yards behind an RAF mosquito fighter-bomber. Rich Welsh voices screamed the orders. Acrid brown smoke drifted over the firing point, obscuring the bright summer sun and the glimmering sea. The Australian pilot of the aircraft encouraged us by giving a running commentary over a loud-speaker system. In the hot stuffy radar wagons, the operators followed every move of the little green blips, which showed the path of aircraft and target. It was the operator's job to 'lock on' the rearward blip, which was the moving sleeve, and thus direct the gunfire. We were a mixed unit and thus it was not uncommon for the male controllers to arrange their shift to be done with a female of their choice. By coincidence a red lamp glowed outside each wagon during firing, prohibiting sudden entrance which would spoil the operator's night vision! Under these darkened conditions, and with a pretty girl beside you, it is easy to imagine how even the most ardent gunner's attention might wander.

'You're dropping short, Cobber. Wow, that's a good 'un,' came our pilot's voice, as his mosquito droned to and fro.

The Lord Lieutenant, enjoying the sun, smoke and stench of cordite, watched as the regiment sweated in the summer's heat. Everything was going terribly well and it must only be a matter of time before someone actually struck the sleeve. Simond's beer tent was sited conveniently near and cool ale awaited the traditional celebration that would follow a direct hit.

Perhaps the heat in the radar wagon had grown too intense or Private Jones too passionate; we never knew. Suddenly the mosquito disappeared amidst a welter of shell bursts.

'Cease fire, cease fire,' shrieked the safety officers, as the plane began to spiral downwards.

The loud-speaker system had gone silent; then, to our intense relief, the Australian pilot spoke. Most of what he actually said is unprintable, but he ended, 'Remember I'm pulling this f—— thing, not pushing it.'

'How about some gin, sir?' said our quick-witted colonel.

The official party stomped off to the mess, whilst the gunners tittered and the Australian managed to land his plane, full of holes, on a nearby airstrip.

However – although on one occasion, when firing in thick fog, we shot up a beauty spot on the Welsh coast and on another sank a fishing boat – it was not our gunnery that worried the authorities as much as our extramural activities. In our midst were many characters who, having tasted both the terror and excitement of real war, found it difficult to settle down to a quiet, sober life. There is a famous tale of a bunch of rascals driving back to camp one evening. They sought to buy some cigarettes from a sea-front kiosk. The little old lady was just closing and refused to serve them. Perhaps unwisely, she commented that they had been drinking and she would never oblige such villains. Their craving unsatisfied and their pride wounded, the six gunners lifted the kiosk, old lady and all, bodily into the back of their truck and, having driven up a rough mountain track, deposited their load 1000 feet above sea level. The poor woman was liberated by a shepherd at dawn and lived to tell her story to the magistrate, who took a very dim view of the whole affair. The gunners explained that they had thought she was asking for a lift and, as they couldn't quite understand what she was saying from within her closed kiosk, they must have got it wrong. 'Guilty,' hooted the indignant beak and the press had a field-day, but strangely, in those days, it only enhanced the regiment's reputation.

One of our camps was plagued with rats coming from a corporation tip on the outskirts of a small town. I was appointed the rodent NCO and, armed with a Sten gun and a torch, did nightly battle with the loathsome creatures on the stinking dump. However, although I expended a fair quantity of ammunition, it was to little avail, and I decided on more drastic action. Approximately sixty pounds of rather old gun cotton had been lying around the stores for several years and the regimental quartermaster sergeant was delighted to be rid of it. I spent a whole day burying the explosive in the centre of the tip. With all the noise of gunfire, I reckoned one more bang would not be noticed, and as the rats were most active after dark, I awaited a night exercise before touching off the charge. To my consternation, the blinding flash and the thundering roar were much more spectacular than any gunfire. Refuse and rats rained down for almost 1000 yards, as I hastened away from the scene. Passing the village chapel next morning, I was surprised to find the preacher standing in the road pointing to the dead rodents that festooned the chapel roof and cemetery. 'A message from Heaven,' he was proclaiming with religious fervour.

It was fortunate that I spent time at each level of rank in the regiment. Although today, soldiers' living conditions have improved out of all recognition, I believe it is no bad thing for officers to do a period of basic training under the same discipline and in the same accommodation as the men they will eventually command. I finished up as an honorary member of the sergeants' mess, where I learnt a very great deal and one important lesson: no matter how good our officers, the warrant officers and the non-commissioned officers are the backbone of the British Army.

But I soon lost my honorary sergeant's stripes and became a private once more. This time it was at the Mecca I had long sought – Sandhurst. The basic training wing brought one down to earth with a bump and we did all those useful character-building activities like floor-scrubbing, boot-bulling, spud-bashing, bed-packing and cutting grass with nail scissors,

Cursed, chased and screamed at by baying drill sergeants, we learnt and re-learnt our military skills for sixteen weeks; until, suddenly, we were officer cadets and fit to enter the Academy proper. Now we were cursed, chased and screamed at by more senior officer cadets and thus the process started again. But if you survived, and most did, you came away from that famous establishment with its motto, 'Serve to lead', firmly fixed in your mind. It was a grand finishing school, often likened to a third-rate university where the Officers' Training Corps had been allowed to run wild.

The bright lights of London were a great lure and, as we moved into our senior terms, there was increased freedom permitting frequent trips to the capital. By working hard one summer leave, I managed to earn enough to buy a Triumph motor-cycle, which worried my parents so much that they quickly helped me to purchase a bone-shaking old sports car. 'Rigormortis' was far more lethal than the motor-bike but, because it had four wheels, was considered safer. 'Don't laugh, Madam, your daughter may be inside', proclaimed a notice on the boot. Indeed, some of my girlfriends' parents were so horrified by the machine that they gladly lent me their own cars for evenings out.

A family friend with a reputation for wild living was quick to understand the pressing needs of a Sandhurst cadet.

'Wouldn't it help if you had a flat in town?' he inquired after a good dinner. 'My company has one in Jermyn Street. We don't use it much and it's always free at weekends.'

I accepted the offer with alacrity and thus began a splendid era of orgies that Rosa Lewis, in whose famous Cavendish Hotel the apartment lay, would have approved.

Arriving back at Sandhurst late one night by taxi, having missed the last train from London, a friend of mine was paying the cabby.

'Nice place you've got here, guv,' remarked the man, who had rarely travelled south of Staines, as they stood in front of the illuminated grand entrance.

'Yes, but it's hell to heat,' said the young man, skipping up the steps.

In 1957 I managed to persuade the Royal Engineers to accept me and thus continued my adventurous life-style. I quickly discovered that sappers lived up to their reputation of being 'Methodist, married and mad' and although the stories of my early days in that illustrious corps are legion, most have been told before.*

By 1958 I was hotly pursuing an attractive and forceful brunette in a stop–go love affair. This in itself became quite an adventure and even involved a forty-two-day circuit of the world, before I was posted to Cyprus for my first taste of active service. There I saw tragedy and glory but, of course, one tends to forget the bad times.

However, it was here that the expeditions really began; diving for antiquities beneath the sea and sorties into the little-known Sahara fulfilled my wildest dreams. Sappers are known as professional obstacle-breakers and we were in much demand to take on a host of exciting tasks.

In 1960 I caught up with the brunette at last and Judith and I were married in time for her to join me for a final blissful year on that Mediterranean island, where peace now reigned. But all good things come to an end, and on Christmas Eve 1961 we landed in Dover in an overladen open sports car, having driven home via Greece and Yugoslavia in freezing weather with no heater and only brandy to keep us warm.

My new job was to train young sappers at the Junior Leaders' Regiment, Royal Engineers, and it didn't please me one bit. However, I quickly found there was lots of fun to be had and learned the vital importance of giving youngsters similar opportunities as those I had enjoyed. In January 1962 I was sent as a temporary instructor to the Outward Bound School at Ullswater. The civilian organization did not appeal at first, but by giving me a new insight into the whole business of character training, it led me to change my ideas which, I think in retrospect, had been rather selfish. It also firmly established my links with the Outward Bound Trust, an organization which I consider to be one of the great success stories of the century. It was something that the Warden at Ullswater wrote about me that caught the eye of the well-known sapper, Colonel (later Major-General) John Cowtan, who was then the senior Royal Engineer at Sandhurst, and in 1963 I was invited to return to my former haunts as an instructor – poacher turned gamekeeper!

The Army had started a new scheme of adventure training and it was my good fortune to be given the responsibility for

* *Where the Trails Run Out* (Hutchinson, 1974).

sending officer cadets all over the globe on expeditions to improve their characters, with the least possible detriment to Britain's foreign relations. No easy task, but it was a wonderful job and a map of the world hanging on my office wall was headed, 'Training Area'. In three and a half years we launched some sixty expeditions of various size and, of course, I often went myself. There were some awful nonsenses as the young men learnt by their mistakes and the mere mention of my name was often sufficient for British defence attachés to take long leave. Nevertheless, there were also many notable successes and, in general, we achieved our aim.

An interesting spin-off from these projects was the liaison established with scientific bodies, for whom the cadets carried out simple tasks. However, not all soldiers appreciated being ordered to collect creepy crawlies and I remember one occasion, in a remote corner of Africa, when an extremely idle driver was left with our Land-Rovers whilst I was away on a lengthy foot patrol.

'While I'm gone, you're not to sit around doing nothing,' I told him. 'The local frogs are of great interest to the British Museum, and I want you to collect as many as possible.'

His face portrayed absolutely no enthusiasm for wading about in a nearby mosquito-infested swamp, catching reptiles. However, he nodded sullenly and I left.

Imagine my surprise when I returned to find the specimen boxes full of frogs!

'How on earth did you do it?' I exclaimed.

'Oh, it was nowt,' replied the driver with unusual modesty. 'You've just got to understand frogs, talk to 'em like,' and, giving vent to a belching sound, he claimed it was the mating cry of the male.

It was many months later that I discovered how this feat and others like it had been achieved, when I saw a photograph taken on the expedition. It showed a smiling soldier giving wide-eyed tribesmen a glance at the centre pages of *Playboy*. 'Two frogs for ten seconds!'

Living in Camberley we were surrounded by wildlife. Urban-dwelling foxes and grey squirrels drove our yellow labrador mad, and a friend of Judith's had quite a frightening encounter. The lady in question had only recently moved into the house when she was awoken one night by the sound of movement in the bedroom. There was no mistaking it, so she roused her husband, who couldn't hear anything, but reluctantly switched on the light.

'There, no one about,' he grunted. 'For goodness' sake, go back to sleep.'

The next night the wife awoke to hear the noises once again. Her husband's temper was not at its best after another fruitless search. When it happened on the third occasion, the poor woman thought she must be out of her mind. However, rather than risk her husband's wrath, she reached out of bed for a torch that she had placed on the floor. As her hand descended, it met something that moved, something that was warm and something that gripped. How she stopped herself screaming, she never knew, but she did and, reaching out with the other hand, found the light switch and turned it on. Holding her fingers was a strange grey furry creature with huge round brown eyes. It was a bushbaby that the previous tenants had lost and, being nocturnal, only appeared after dark!

In 1967, after three and a half happy years at Sandhurst, we had to move on. My friend, Colonel (later Brigadier) Tony Landale, had just been appointed Commander Royal Engineers of the 3rd Division at Tidworth. We both enjoyed shooting and loved labradors, so I was delighted when he asked me to be his adjutant. It was while I was in this job that His Imperial Majesty Haile Selassie's request to explore his Blue Nile was followed up and I was lucky to be given every possible encouragement by the Army to carry out this mammoth task. However, whilst the preparation got under way, the Ministry of Defence decreed that, having passed my Staff College entrance exam, I must go to the Royal Military College of Science for fifteen months before doing the year at Camberley. The thought of going back to school again filled me with horror and indeed it was only made bearable by the fiery commandant, Major-General (later Lieutenant-General Sir) Napier Crookenden, who told me to get on with the running of the expedition and not worry too much about calculus and chemistry!

The Blue Nile, or Great Abbai as it is called in Ethiopia, plunges for 500 miles through the highlands of Ethiopia and runs through a gorge, which in many places is over one mile deep.

All previous attempts to explore this little-known region had failed, but in July 1968 we launched a seventy-strong Anglo-

Ethiopian team of servicemen and civilians to carry out scientific research along this infamous valley. After an initial recce I returned to Britain in time to explain the project to Her Majesty the Queen and His Royal Highness Prince Philip during their visit to the Royal School of Military Engineering. HRH seemed especially interested in the venture and offered some good advice on the design of our craft.

To study the river, we planned to move by boat in the wet season, when the flood-water should smooth out the cataracts. The lower reaches would be covered first and then the more dangerous headwaters would be tackled. There were other hazards, including crocodiles, hippos and disease, but the major problem was that of resupply. This was overcome by parachute drops from an Army Beaver aircraft, flown specially from Britain.

The scientists included archaeologists, a veterinary surgeon and five zoologists. A Bilharzia survey and geological studies were undertaken, whilst game and crocodile surveys were made for the Ethiopian wildlife department. Although the three services gave considerable support, we still had to find £15 000 to pay for the expedition. This in itself was a task almost as difficult as the navigation of the river. However, as on all our trips, members paid for the honour of coming and somehow we raised the money.

In late July we established the main base at Debra Marcos in the Goggam highlands of Ethiopia and then set out from Shafartak in four Royal Engineer assault craft, with modifications as suggested by Prince Philip.

For three weeks we battled through the cataracts of the mighty river, stopping at selected points for scientific work. Specimens were taken out of the gorge by mule parties, who likened their journey to the ascent of a never-ending ladder in a Turkish bath. The steep slopes were covered in loose rocks, concealed by elephant grass up to twelve feet high. Midday temperatures could soar to around 90°F and the humidity could go to 85 per cent. The final phase of the expedition was the descent from Lake Tana to Shafartak. The first fifty miles were obstructed by raging white-water cataracts and the river party moved in special Avon inflatable boats. We were all novices at this game, learning as we went. Looking back on those days it is interesting that all our river-exploring techniques developed from that expedition.

The voyage was an extreme test of men and equipment and, tragically, one of our soldiers was drowned whilst crossing a tributary. The final descent was through a completely unexplored gorge. Here there were more crocodiles, and cataracts that could not be bypassed. In three days we negotiated twelve major rapids, fought two gun battles with bandit gangs and met many large crocodiles. We sailed through fantastic, vertical-sided canyons and saw a land that no other white men had seen before. Indeed these days are a story in themselves.*

The expedition lost much of its equipment and several boats, and had 50 per cent casualties of one sort or another. Nevertheless, we managed to cross the finishing line on 24 September, a little under two months after we had set out. As our boats approached the great bridge at Shafartak they were dwarfed by the magnitude of the gorge, but it was a proud sight as we sailed in flying the flags of Britain and Ethiopia.

The expedition had been strongly supported by the *Daily Telegraph* and we owed much to our friends there for the good publicity that we got throughout the world. Anglia Television edited and distributed our film and in all the expedition was a tremendous success.

There was no doubt that we had something worth keeping and so the following year the members of our team formed the Scientific Exploration Society, which aims to organize and encourage scientific exploration world-wide. It is this organization that has now become the driving force behind many major expeditions.

Having cracked that nut, I found it extremely difficult to settle down to mundane study again and already I was planning another expedition. The Staff College at Camberley was more enjoyable than Shrivenham, but I still needed extra excitement to keep me going. I'd popped across for lunch with my old chums at Sandhurst one day, when I bumped into the beaming Brigadier Peter Young.

'Good morrow, Blashford,' he roared, slapping me on the back. 'You're the sort of man who likes a fight and enjoys a spot of rape, loot and pillage – I've got a job for you!'

* Richard Snailham, *The Blue Nile Revealed* (Chatto & Windus, 1970).

2. Living history

The King's army was crossing the open ground some 600 yards to my front. In the summer's sunlight the cavalry, infantry and camp-followers of the Royalist forces were a colourful sight. The breeze carried the sound of drum and fife as well as the oaths of the gunners who were coming into view, sweating on the drag ropes as they heaved the great culverins over the ankle-deep grass.

Sir William Waller, my commanding officer, dressed in puritan black with his hand resting on a fine silver-embellished pistol, watched them too. He glanced casually towards the clump of trees where I sat upon the sixteen-hand grey charger, and nodded. I acknowledged the signal and, turning about, cantered to the rear, rounded a leafy bush and faced my Ironsides.

Sixty or so stood by their horses, their black lobster helmets glinting, orange sashes standing out against their drab leather coats. There was not a cigarette, not a pair of dark glasses, not a wrist-watch, nor indeed any vestige of the twentieth century.

'Ironsides, mount,' I yelled, and at once the troopers sprang into the saddle.

'Captain Muir,' I shouted. 'Pray advance the horse beyond yonder ditch, whence you will see the malignant host. Then thou shalt take them in the flank, for they do presume to cross our front.'

'It shall be so, sir,' replied the young cavalry commander.

'We'll ride with you,' I called as the horses began to move.

'On the right, then,' replied the good Captain Muir.

As we came out from the cover of the trees, the Ironsides shook out into a box formation, some five ranks of twelve.

'Draw swords,' came the order.

Visors dropped and we splashed through a shallow brook, passed through the gaps in the hedge and entered a large meadow, at the far end of which the enemy was still moving slowly to the east. They saw us at once and when we were still 400 yards from them, trotting forward in good order, they began to run out cannon and form square. I could see Prince Rupert's cavalry behind the Foote, trying to find a gap in the confused ranks through which they could come out to meet us.

'Ironsides, charge,' screamed Johnnie Muir.

At once every trooper brought the flat of his blade down on the rump of the horse in front. The tight box of cavalry rocketed ahead with the thunder of hooves. We bent forward, grateful for the wind that cooled. To stand in even forty pounds of armour, leather and thigh boots is no joke on a summer's day.

The King's coach was making to the rear and already some of the better-drilled regiments had formed square, impenetrable forests of pikes, when the cannon opened on us. Puffs of white smoke heralded the hiss of the first ball to pass over.

'Too high,' we laughed, but the next whizzed between us and struck a trooper, who went down, horse and all, among the flying hooves.

A thin line of Royalist cavalry galloped to meet us. Spumes of sweat and foam flicked back from my grey's mouth. Each animal seemed determined to outpace the next. The speed was frightening. Now the two bodies of horse were closing at nearly seventy miles per hour and, seconds later, came the crash of the impact. In the whirling kaleidoscope of colour, two Cavaliers were pitched from the saddle in front of me. We leapt over sprawling bodies, brushed a riderless horse aside and collided with a short, fat fellow who, having lost his sword, was trying to draw his pistol. The combined blow of sixteen hands of grey and sixteen stone of me sent the man and his mount rolling over in the lush grass.

A glancing blow on my helmet made me look left. A Cavalier officer, beautifully attired in claret corduroy and white lace, was hacking at me with his sword. Almost stationary, I reached out with my far longer blade and deftly removed his hat. Thus dismayed, he backed away, only to be struck by another oncoming Ironside.

'On, on, on, through,' Johnnie was yelling.

So, digging my heels in, I quickly left the unseemly tangle of men and horses and charged on into the acrid smoke.

The formation, in which we had started this mad steeple-chase, was no more. Half our number was down or still engaged with Prince Rupert's men. Now joined by a dozen riderless horses, we plunged towards the tightly packed infantry. Fifty yards out came the order, 'Pistols!' My comrades drew their weapons and fired a volley at the pikemen. Alas, my grey, my aide-de-camp's palamino and the riderless horses were just beginning to enjoy the fun. Pull as I might, I could not stop. Seeing the horses coming, a faint-hearted foot-soldier dropped his pike and fled. We poured through the gap. The twelve-foot spears waved towards us, but then suddenly we were behind the line. Two or three maids and a page fled in terror from us. A gallant gunner raised a musket; it misfired and he caught an awful blow from my ADC's sword.

Screaming like banshees, we scattered two gun crews, kicking over powder barrels and slashing down a standard, before whirling right to circle behind the enemy and rejoin our friends. What tremendous fun, the wildest schoolboy dream come true!

'Ow!' I spat, as something very hard hit my upper arm a stinging blow. 'What the hell was that?'

'A tennis ball, my lord – one of ours,' said Frances Copping, my ADC, raising her visor and mopping the perspiration from her brow. Sure enough, in the middle distance the line of trees where we had started was masked now by drifting clouds of smoke, as the Roundhead artillery engaged the army of King Charles.

With the same infinite care as he had designed the Nocra Hilton on our Dahlak Island Expedition in 1969, Gerald Batt laid his 'Long Tom'.

'There,' he said, 'let's see how they like this – Fire!'

Propelled by a thunderflash, a tennis ball whistled down the meadow. His earlier shots had all been high, but this ball struck a small enemy cannon, whose fuse was already burning, on the wheel. The gun spun around and discharged itself at its crew and a great cheer went up from the Army of the Lord, as we sometimes called ourselves. Cromwell's men were enjoying the artillery duel. Gerald's next shot hit the breech of an enemy culverin and bounced about amongst the gun crew, causing a standard-bearer to drop his colours. Thus encouraged, the vicar general ordered the Twenty-third Psalm (to Crimmond) and the Roundheads gave tongue.

The final act of the day was the inevitable head-on clash of the Foote – as chance would have it, on a narrow bridge. The cavalry stood back as the rival mobs, no regimental order remaining, beat hell out of each other! One poor fellow lost his teeth to a pike butt – 'Well, he shouldn't have joined if he couldn't take a joke,' commented Sir William (alias author and historian Dr John Adair).

Eventually the stentorian bellow of ex-commando Brigadier Peter Young, captain general of the Sealed Knot, brought a stop to the blood-bath. We all shook hands and limped back to our respective camps. The 5000 spectators trooped home, having had twenty-pence-worth of fun. Local charity benefited and the good people of Cropredy breathed a sigh of relief!

Brigadier Peter had formed the Sealed Knot in the spring of 1968 when, following the publication of his book on the Battle of Edgehill, he realized the enormous interest and enthusiasm that existed for this sanguine but important time in our history. The original society of the Sealed Knot was a secret organization of Royalist sympathizers, which plotted to bring about the restoration of the monarchy after the execution of King Charles.

In no time the brigadier, a noted military historian and expert on the Civil War, had formed an army. Many of his friends, always ready for a spot of colourful fun, joined the ranks and by October 1968 he was able to muster a sizable force to re-create the Battle of Edgehill. The day was a great success, but all agreed it lacked one essential – the enemy. The severe puritan habit and less extravagant ways of the Roundheads did not at first appeal to the masses, who were prepared to give up their summer weekends to indulge in a little warfare.

However, the wily brigadier, who in his earlier days had stormed the beaches at Dieppe, saw no problem in this and in time persuaded his modest colleague, John Adair, to form the Roundhead Association. Knowing my fascination for explosives and hearing me remark that I was descended from Cromwell, the brigadier immediately made me a 'Colonel of the Parliamentary Engineers', on condition that I would provide a realistic pyrotechnic display at his next battle.

My explosive efforts at Basing House won wide acclaim, even if one of my devices almost hit my old friend John Wilsey, who was flying overhead in the Sandhurst light aircraft, and another prostrated a young lad in the Royalist army. By the time we met at Marston Moor in June 1970 I had been appointed general of engineers. Promotion is always fast in war.

The Muscat Regiment's mortar platoon four-tonner after striking the mine. Royal Engineer column in the background

The author on the Blue Nile in 1968 with WO2 Ticky Wright RE (centre) and Sgt John Huckstep RE (right). Capt Garth Brocksopp RIR is towed in the Avon

'Bish' as a chaplain in 53rd Welsh Division during World War II

Opposite above: Vampire bats always plagued the horses in the Darien jungle, but in 1976 the author was also attacked by one

Opposite below: Emma, Judith, JB–S and Victoria during an outing from school

Below: The author leads the Army of Parliament against the Royalists at a Sealed Knot battle

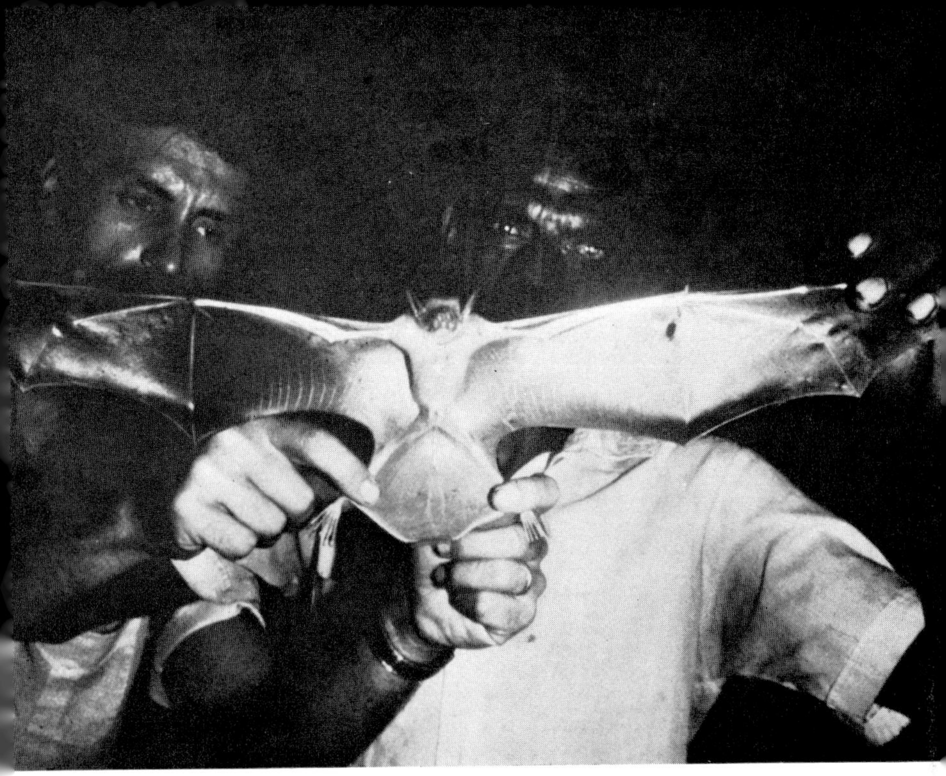

Hit by an IRA mine, a Ferret armoured car burns on an Ulster road. A young officer was killed, but miraculously the driver lived. The author's vehicle was the next one down the road

RAF Harrier Jump Jet thunders into the air from a grass field in West Germany

It was on this Yorkshire field that an extraordinary thing happened. The night before the battle we had the usual administrative problems of assembling our armies. Cannon had to be transported on lorries, powder brought up and securely stored, personnel moved by car, coach and train and, most difficult of all, the horses got to the site. This last load meant convoys of horse boxes; and then the animals had to be exercised, fed, watered, groomed and bedded down. We were especially anxious that they should get a good night's rest in order to be at their best next day.

The same could not be said for our followers who, on arrival, would usually demand ale and entertainment. Thus it was that we had taken over a farmer's barn and it was here at about midnight that I was attempting to check how many of the 'trayne' of artillery and engineers had reached Yorkshire. Outside, the stocks were already full and the Sealed Knot's own provost staff was busy carrying out those who offended our liberal code of behaviour. Cries of 'God Save the King' brought instant replies of 'God and Parliament'. Beer flowed like water and demure young ladies cast inhibitions to the wind and flirted outrageously with men whom they scarcely would have glanced at in twentieth-century garb. It seemed that once we donned our costumes, we left the world of today far behind.

In the centre of it all the beaming captain general sat, at a high table, a goblet of wine gripped in his great hand and a pretty aide at his side. The flamboyance and merriment of the seventeenth century which the Knot was so good at re-creating was in full swing.

'Sir, sir, come quickly, some drunken fools are riding the horses round the battlefield,' yelled a serious-faced young Ironside, who was one of our more reliable officers.

'What!' I bellowed, in genuine rage. 'Who are they?'

'I don't know,' said the officer, 'but those horses will be no use tomorrow and it will be lucky if one doesn't break a leg.'

We rushed outside, joined by two members of the trayne.

'Tom and I were coming across the field from the camp-site a few minutes ago when we heard the horses, at least thirty of them I'd say, coming at the gallop. First of all I thought it was just that they'd broken loose and were running about by themselves. Then we heard the shouts of the riders and realized that they were out there.' The officer pointed towards the moor.

'Did you see them?' I asked.

'Yes, but only fleetingly, I couldn't make out the individuals, but they looked like Cavaliers, with their big hats. Didn't see any of our Roundhead lobster helmets.'

'Bloody idiots,' I cursed. 'You go with one man and stop anyone coming out of that gate, don't go into the field. In the dark you could be trampled. I'll go to the horse lines and see what's happening there.'

So saying, I set off at the run. The horses were tethered in a long meadow on the edge of Marston Moor. The night was pitch-black, with only a slight wind. 'Funny,' I thought, 'can't hear anything.' The horse boxes loomed up in the gloom.

I found a sleepy stable lad who came stumbling with me, torch in hand. He flicked the beam down the meadow. Forty pairs of green eyes looked back.

'They looks all right,' he said.

We checked the other horses too. In disbelief, I felt the flanks of several – cold.

'Thank you,' I muttered, 'sorry to get you up.'

I walked slowly on to the battlefield. A mist was rising from the marshy ground. I listened for five minutes; there was no sound, except perhaps once I thought I heard something, very faint, very very faint indeed, but not horses – just a distant cacophony of sounds. I could not be sure. How much ale had I drunk? I turned to walk back to the barn and suddenly I felt terribly cold, yet I was clad in many layers and wore a heavy black cloak. The party was dying down.

'Ah ha! The Lord Protector himself,' roared a gang of jolly Cavaliers.

'Aye, and looking right glum,' said another. 'Have a drink, John.'

'Yes, thank you,' I said, removing my helmet. 'A glass of your rum would go down very well.'

Beneath all the amusement, there was a serious purpose to our activities. By restaging the battles on the original ground and using authentic equipment, those of us interested in the history of warfare could appreciate the difficulties faced by the forces from which developed the modern British Army.

Both Roundheads and Cavaliers had regiments of horse, foot, dragoons and traynes of artillery. Our membership included people from every walk of life, with a wide variety of jobs. Regular soldiers were much in evidence, but we also had dealers in antique weapons, fashion photographers, metal workers, lawyers, carpenters, doctors, business executives, secretaries and lorry drivers. Girls fought as men and acted as camp followers; on the Roundhead side, Judith and Kay Thompson organized a nursing corps, known as the Sisters of Chastity! Alas Judith was later dismissed for drinking wine upon the field of battle.

Recruiting was no problem. Those with the sense of the theatrical obviously preferred being Cavaliers, for the glorious uniforms, if nothing else. Although the simple, more modest armour and leather of the Roundheads had a definite appeal and was certainly less expensive. The recruiters for the Army of the Covenant were ever ready to point out that many very attractive damsels rode with the Royalist cavalry 'and will be yours by right of conquest, for as according to history, we always win'.

The battles were usually staged by request, so that a local charity could benefit from the large crowds that flocked to see the carnage. Was this not the attitude of Rome in its period of decline? However, although our casualties were not uncommon, they were rarely serious. One attractive wench was carried off to hospital at Plymouth with a strained back.

'How did you do this?' questioned the doctor.

'Well, I had to be raped by a Roundhead,' she explained, 'but whilst trying to catch me, he fell off his horse and squashed me flat.'

When it is remembered that officers had no real authority, discipline was surprisingly good, although we always considered the Cavaliers rather unruly and issued strict warnings to our Ironsides against 'brawling, duelling, bear- and bull-baiting'.

At the re-enactment of the first battle of Newbury (20 September 1643) I found myself acting the part of Sir John Merrick, whose Parliamentary artillery played an important part in the battle. Being rather short of officers, I persuaded a dozen fellow students from the Staff College to join for the day. Amongst them was a United States Army major, George Smolenyak, who had recently fought in Vietnam. George, dressed as a puritan officer, was in the thick of the fight during which his fibre-glass helmet was topped by a Cavalier's sword! Emerging battered, bruised and truncated, George was heard to mutter, 'Gee, Vietnam was never as dangerous as this!'

In Jersey, fellow sapper officer, Graham Fawcus, and I

besieged Gorey Castle on behalf of the Lion's Club and caused havoc in a crowded St Helier where a highly strung horse jumped through the back window of a parked car and a troop of Ironsides brushed an old lady off her garden wall to land inverted, with legs kicking, in a rose bed. At St Ouens Bay we re-created what I believe was the first amphibious landing by the British Army against a hostile coastline at night. History records that it was here that the Parliamentary army under Colonel James Heane landed from lighters at midnight on 22 October 1651 and, after a fierce battle with the Jersey Royalist cavalry, established a beach-head.

For the re-enactment we were provided with some splendid thoroughbreds from a local stables. These were not the gun-trained beasts that we used in England and I had just mounted a powerfully built grey and was adjusting my stirrups when the animal reared up. Alas, I had forgotten to remove the roll spurs we wore for show and had unintentionally dug one in. Now there was no holding the furious animal and, having attempted to throw me, he set off at a breakneck gallop up St Ouens Beach, which is five miles long. I did my uttermost to keep the spurs away from him, but it was not easy at that speed.

'Turn his head,' shouted my friends, as I disappeared.

After about 500 yards, I managed to do this and back we raced. I swept past the army, who cheered loudly as I threw away all the accoutrements that I felt would do me harm when I eventually came off. No matter how hard I pulled, the horse would not stop, but, if anything, went faster. A low break-water lay ahead. Not being a terribly proficient horseman, I prepared for the worst, but with amazing ease, we cleared the weed-coated timbers and raced on. Again I turned him and again we passed the army – more ribald remarks!

'How stupid,' I thought, 'but I simply cannot stop this creature, the only way is to ride him to exhaustion.'

At that moment, without warning, he turned sharp right and we parted company. I hit the sand on my head and back, knocking all the wind out of myself. I lay there, gasping for breath. My back felt numb, but, to my astonishment, I was able to move my limbs. As I started to rise painfully to my feet I heard a snort behind and looked round to see my tormentor standing over me. Seeing the blood on his flanks, I at once forgot my own distress and, taking the reins, spoke softly to the poor chap for a few minutes. Meanwhile, I discovered my only injury from the fall was a cut on my nose from the visor; otherwise the fibre-glass armour and helmet had protected me. Two Ironsides galloped up.

'Are you OK?'

'As far as I can tell,' I said and, removing my spurs, remounted and trotted down the beach to join in the battle at the water's edge.

My last act with the Sealed Knot was to put the old Shropshire town of Ludlow to the sword. It was a fine summer's afternoon when Graham Fawcus and I laid siege to the castle as part of the Ludlow Festival. The Parliamentary headquarters was in Ye Olde Feathers Hotel and our council of war was held in an upper room that had certainly been there at the time of the battle.

We placed the Roundhead cannon at the exact spot where they had stood originally and, to make a really good spectacle, carried out an assault on the walls using ingenious re-creations of the engines of war, although in reality the castle had surrendered. Shortly before the battle commenced a Cromwellian regiment arrived late. We had sufficient attackers, whilst Brigadier Peter, defending the castle, was rather short-handed, so I ordered the latecomers to change sides and join the Royalists.

'We don't believe in monarchy,' stated one of their lieutenants. 'We'll only fight as Roundheads.'

I called him aside.

'Listen to me,' I said sternly. 'I may be sitting on a horse, playing the part of a Parliamentary general, and I understand that Cromwell was an ancestor of mine, but in real life I am an officer of the Queen. We are only actors in a pageant and if you feel otherwise you should not be here. Go and do as you're told or leave now.'

The disgruntled regiment shuffled off to report to the brigadier in the castle and doubtless complained bitterly that Blashford-Snell had been unreasonable. Peter Young was at his most cunning and posted them to hold the sallyport whence, although they knew it not, my main attack was to come. So it was that an hour later they were blasted by the cannon of our siege machine, 'the Great Sow', and then trampled underfoot by our best infantry. So perish all. . . .

Nevertheless, this incident forewarned me that a small minority of members were getting a little too serious about the whole thing. There was no doubt that the Sealed Knot was the greatest fun. It was good exercise, hard work and a form of escape from the times in which we live. But the enormous burden of administrating the Roundheads was regularly falling on the same people and I simply could not devote the time required. But my love of fancy dress did continue.

We have always managed to give unusual parties and in 1970 Judith and Diana Fawcus thought up the idea of a Viking Blot. Apparently this was an early Scandinavian drinking orgy and fertility rights. We selected Hawley Lake, the Royal Engineers watermanship training area in Hampshire, as the venue, set up a marquee – just in case it rained – and hired an extraordinary all-electric musical group equipped with a sort of portable water organ. We decked out two thirty-five-foot whalers as Viking ships and moved in a vast quantity of wine.

Whilst we were setting this up, the Sealed Knot was amusing the crowds at the Sandhurst Horse Show. At the height of the battle, our friend Ken Monck, playing his usual part of the vicar general and extolling the Roundheads to spare no one, but to do the Lord's work and smite the malignants with all their might, was ridden down by a Cavalier. Looking much the worse for wear, poor Kenneth was carried off the field to a waiting Army ambulance. The Royal Army Medical Corps corporal took a quick look and decided that hospital was the answer, so when Ken came to his senses he was at the Cambridge Military Hospital in Aldershot.

'Rank?' inquired the orderly.

'Vicar general,' groaned Kenneth.

'Name, sir?' said the soldier with new respect.

'Monck,' replied Kenneth.

'Date of injury?'

'11 September 1646,' said Ken.

'How exactly did it happen?' said the orderly, more than a little puzzled.

'Ridden down in a charge of cavalry,' said Ken, in his soft Welsh voice.

Looking at the form, the orderly summed it all up in the remarks column, 'Mind wandering. Suspect brain damage', and sent him off for head X-ray.

It was nearly 2230 hours before the hospital finished setting his broken arm and Ken was able to change into his costume of the High Priest of Wodon and persuade the army to dispatch him by ambulance to the scene of the orgy. The dancing girls, a dozen nubile nymphs fresh from being 'raped' on the Sandhurst lawns in the cause of charity, were now attired in sealskin bikinis and cavorting in an erotic dance that set the men's pulses racing. Just as Ken arrived, a duel resulted in one guest being run through the hand with a sword, so the ambulance did not have a wasted return trip.

As the specially imported and extra strong Danish beer flowed, the party really got into its stride. The Viking ships raced up and down the lake. A few guests who had foolishly come in suits of chain-mail almost drowned. Finally we auctioned the slave girls for the Benevolent Fund and, as a thick mist descended on the lake, the party dissolved into chaos as guests tried to find parked cars and, having done so, attempted to drive them.

Partly for reasons of security, I decided to spend what remained of the night on the site and collapsed on to a great bearskin in the marquee. I awoke at dawn, very stiff, with a wicked headache and, stepping over my many prostrate friends, staggered out. Around me was a terrible scene of desolation. Broken weapons, sealskin bikinis, Viking regalia and empty bottles. The smoke from the fires drifted vertically upwards in the still air and beyond I could see the Viking ships, one demasted, riding at anchor on the misty lake.

Seeking some privacy to attend to the most pressing business of the moment, I strolled off into the rhododendrons. Still dressed as Wodon, with two-horned helmet, beard, cloak, skins and sword, I was eagerly watering the flowers when I sensed I was not alone. Looking up quickly, I saw a wide-eyed, bespectacled fisherman, complete with green waders, landing net and rod, gaping at me from twenty yards off. His Jack Russell, one leg raised, also stared.

'What ho!' I bellowed, waving my sword with my free hand.

To my amazement, the poor fellow turned and fled. I often wonder what he told his psychiatrist!

3. Busy years

At the end of 1969 I finished my Staff College course and managed to fit in a quick expedition to the Ethiopian Dahlak Islands in the Red Sea before taking up a new appointment in Whitehall. Although the idea of pushing paper in the Ministry of Defence did not greatly appeal to me, I soon discovered that if one was to survive it was vital to understand the workings of the Civil Service. I found that if handled correctly this much-maligned body of dedicated people could really be most helpful.

Of course not all the military officers at the ministry could achieve a good working rapport with their civilian opposite numbers. One young cavalryman found himself in deep trouble whilst attempting to oil the wheels of a conference dealing with the defence estimates, by ordering chocolate biscuits for coffee break. His claim to the finance branch for ten pence was rejected out of hand with the comment, 'Biscuits, chocolate, are for generals. Other officers only qualify for biscuits, plain.'

There were countless files to be studied and many had been in circulation for decades. One which was often read for light amusement, concerned a claim for compensation from an irate householder who complained of a wartime concrete bunker, complete with coastal artillery piece, that was still in his garden. As a housing estate had grown up around the weapon he pointed out that to fire it would certainly cause fatal casualties amongst the population of Little Piddling-on-Sea and he demanded that we should remove it or pay heavy compensation. The correspondence had flowed since June 1945 and one could trace the steady decline in the poor fellow's sanity. The ministry letters were sympathetic, but unhelpful. Sometimes they blamed the economy, sometimes another ministry and finally the local council for having erected houses around the gun emplacement. However, offers of help were made from time to time such as, 'The matter is under review by the engineer-in-chief and it is hoped that the defences in question may be demolished by explosive charges with the minimum damage to your property', or 'As the removal of the block-house is now considered impractical perhaps you would wish to make an offer to purchase it.'

There was the usual crop of letters to the Member of Parliament concerned and about once every twelve months a really abusive one from the tortured victim himself. It was interesting to note that when this happened the ministry rolled itself up, hedgehog-like, in a protective ball and refused to reply, thus forcing the complainant to eat humble pie and write an obsequious plea to obtain an answer. Of course, staff officers changed every two years and so the ministry was constantly being revitalized whilst the householder's health declined. When he finally expired a loose minute on the file suggested that the matter should now be passed to the antiquities department of the Ministry of Public Buildings and Works.

Not all officers posted to Whitehall had exciting and challenging staff jobs. One colleague, who was shortly to leave the Army, was given a really boring appointment. A major part of his work was to rewrite the emergency standing orders for action to be taken in the event of the River Thames flooding Westminster. The task was truly formidable and would involve months of toil. Gloomily my friend started work and each day he grew more miserable. However, inspiration came to him as he strolled passed Ladbrokes on his way home one evening. He only hesitated for a second, then, popping into the betting shop, inquired what odds they would give against the Thames flooding in the next six months. The clerk made a quick phone call to head office and announced with pride that the chances were considered to be one thousand to one. Next day the staff officer placed a £20 bet and hurled the loathsome files into his cupboard saying, 'Well, even if I'm court-martialled, I'll be rich.'

Occasionally there were bitter scenes of inter-service rivalry and I recall a dreadful moment when a fleet-footed senior airman seized the last of the prized cream doughnuts from the tea trolley which a lady of West African origin trundled round the corridors of power. Alas, a great splodge of jam and synthetic cream shot from the confectionery right on to the highly polished toecap of a peppery brigadier.

There were lovable characters too. These included the gentleman who controlled the procurement and provision of mobile laundry and bath units for the British Army, whose proud boast was that he'd washed ten million men since D-Day, and the lady who made the office coffee, who would present you with a chipped and stained mug on your first day saying, 'There you are dearie, General Foresight had that when 'e was 'ere as a major. Bring you luck it will.' It did, and I needed it, for most of my second year in Whitehall was spent planning the British Trans-Americas Expedition in a basement room of the Old War Office. Here I spent long hours after everyone else had gone, slaving away at our plans. Mrs Lee, a humorous cleaner, would mop up around me and say, 'Don't you ever go home?'

This massive expedition aimed to focus publicity on the need to complete the Pan-American Highway, which was interrupted by an unbelievably nasty piece of jungle and swamp in Panama and Colombia called the Darien Gap. Mounted by a London-based committee of persons with an interest in the Americas, and by the Army, the expedition was a real cliff-hanger.

The completion of the Pan-American Highway, a 17000-mile route running from Alaska in the north, through Canada, the United States, Mexico, Central and South America, to Cape Horn in the south, had for a long time been a dream. Breaking that route on the slender isthmus connecting North and South America, which was partly in Panama and partly in Colombia, was some of the most difficult country in the world to penetrate – steaming tropical jungle and weed-choked swamp. Known as the Darien Gap or El Tapon – the 'Stopper' – that unbridged section stretched from Canitas to Barranquillito, and it had in the past defeated all attempts to take vehicles throughout its length.

The idea that yet another expedition should be mounted to overcome this formidable obstacle and so draw attention to the need to complete the highway, came originally from the Darien Action Committee in the Americas and a British Trans-Americas Expedition Committee which was formed in 1970 under the energetic chairmanship of Lieutenant-Colonel Julian du Parc Braham.

Experienced explorers and travellers in this wild land were asked whether they thought such a venture was feasible. Most replied that it was folly, especially as several other well-prepared expeditions had failed. The area, with its countless ravines, rivers and rises, was also infested with such unpleasant creatures as scorpions, hornets, stinging caterpillars, huge ants and spiders, vampire bats and snakes. Mention was also made of the possibility of roving bands of rebels.

For advice on the idea the committee had come to me. My first reaction was that the proposed venture was madness, but after reconnaissance carried out by a young Irish chum of mine, I concluded that it could be done. It would need to be a massive undertaking fought like a long-drawn-out battle, with a good chance of high casualties and a certainty of great discomfort.

The project got under way and its supporters included the British Army, the governments of Panama and Colombia, the British Museum (Natural History), our own Scientific Exploration Society, plus numerous commercial companies and individuals in Britain and the Americas.

With the backing of the Army, and in particular the Royal Engineers, the expedition assumed the proportions of a wartime task force; sixty-four men and women from Britain and the United States joined Panamanian and Colombian servicemen in Central America in early January 1972.

Members of the expedition were picked for their compatibility, physical fitness and expertise. I intended to form a team and not a group of prima donnas and, looking back on it, I reckon I was about 90 per cent successful. They ranged from experienced explorers, mountaineers and jungle experts to a couple of seventeen-year-olds from the Junior Leaders' Regiment, Royal Engineers, who had never been out of Britain previously, and an eighteen-year-old civilian who had just left school. The soldiers in the party were from most regiments and there was no shortage of volunteers. The civilians included a number of American, British and Panamanian scientists who carried out a carefully planned programme. This involved the study of the botany, entomology, geography, geology and zoology of the region, and also of the local Indians and their life.

Air support included a British Army Beaver aircraft and helicopters from the United States Air Force and the air forces of Panama and Colombia; medium-range transport aircraft and light reconnaissance planes also assisted. The vehicles chosen to complete the full 17000-mile, north-to-south drive were two prestigious Range-Rovers kindly provided by

British Leyland. In 1971 they were the world's most up-to-date four-wheel-drive vehicles. These were fitted with motor-driven Fairey capstans for winching, 'cow-catcher' extensions to the bumpers, roof-racks, water tanks and snorkels for deep wading. Each vehicle carried three aluminium ladders on its roof-rack; one carried a special Avon inflatable raft. When small tracked load-carriers finally glued themselves up in the mud, we brought in a Land-Rover pathfinder vehicle, bought in Panama. Each car was crewed by three men. The Range-Rovers finally left Alaska in early December 1971 and reached Cape Horn in June 1972.

But the real story is what happened in the gap.* Twenty-eight ponies, the only available pack animals in Panama, were used to carry stores as far as the Colombian border where, to comply with foot and mouth regulations, they were to be replaced by local mules. The horses played a vital part in enabling the expedition to advance, although, due to disease, sickness and accident, five had to be destroyed or died on the way. Nevertheless, in spite of what all pessimists said, twenty-three survived. This was a great credit to our veterinary officer, Major (now Lieutenant-Colonel) Keith Morgan-Jones, and his animal transport team who worked tirelessly to keep our faithful beasts going.

The rations, largely in dehydrated form, were designed specially for the expedition by the victualling department of the Ministry of Defence, and they were very good. Additional food was provided by numerous kind sponsors and, to economize on the supplies, we also ate local dishes which included wild turkey, fish, iguana, monkey, snakes and, of course, jungle fruit.

Supplies delivered into the jungle during the course of the expedition included ten tons of rations, 15 000 gallons of petrol, 2400 cans of beer and 80 000 cigarettes, sacks of horse fodder, boxes of dynamite and the mail. They were brought in variously by boat, helicopter, parachute and pack horse.

The entire logistic support of the project was organized with great efficiency by my second-in-command, Major Kelvin Kent, who on return to Britain was swiftly dispatched to do the same job for the 1972 British Everest Expedition.

* Russell Braddon's *The Hundred Days of Darien* (Collins, 1974) is the official book of the expedition, and the story is also told in my *Where the Trails Run Out*.

Thirty miles into the gap the Range-Rovers developed serious problems in their differentials, which were only solved in the nick of time by the fantastic efforts made by our friends in the Rover company.

There were times when it was hard to believe that we would ever get through the green hell – but our ragged band pressed indomitably on. Casualties mounted daily and several strong men were so affected by the nervous fatigue of their experiences that they had to be evacuated with what amounted to expedition 'shell-shock'. Undoubtedly logic and common sense would have made us give up many times, but logic and common sense do not come into these circumstances. Courage, determination and endurance were to win through in the end.

With our sweat-soaked clothing in shreds, faces drawn and bodies a mass of bites and sores, the expedition and its vehicles finally linked up with the northern end of the Pan-American Highway's southern section after ninety-nine days of battling against the jungle and swamps of Darien. By coincidence it was St George's Day!

Complete success for the entire project came on 9 June 1972 when a signal arrived from Captain Jeremy Groves, who had taken the Range-Rovers on to Cape Horn: 'Mission accomplished.' The most ambitious expedition that the Army had ever undertaken had been successfully completed, and the sequel was the subsequent announcement that the Pan-American Highway had been allocated the $150 million it needed to follow in our path and bridge El Tapon. In addition, the research and the recommendations made by our scientific section did much to help conserve the fauna and flora of the region and protect the interests of the local Indians.

Fortunately the sale of our special expedition covers and a good crop of lectures soon cleared our debts. However, the diseases that many of us had picked up in that terrible piece of country were to linger on for years to come. Almost weekly we heard of some illness being discovered in one of our members and I myself suffered for eighteen months afterwards with one particular tropical malady which, although fairly minor, was rather uncomfortable. My only regret was that the expedition had been such a severe test of strength and character, from which several members never really recovered.

However, whilst we had been hacking our way through this impenetrable jungle two other members of the Scientific

Exploration Society had been carrying out the initial reconnaissance for the next great venture. Dick Snailham and Martin Romilly had been to Zaire, then still named the Congo, to carry out a feasibility study for the proposed H. M. Stanley Centenary Expedition of 1974. But while Dick and Martin were preparing their reports I had to go back to some routine soldiering and was most fortunate to be given command of the 48th Field Squadron, Royal Engineers, based at Ripon in Yorkshire. I say fortunate because it was an excellent unit. The previous commander had been my friend, Robin Jukes-Hughes, and as we both had similar ideas on life, it meant that I was stepping into a job that had clearly been shaped along lines I was happy to continue.

Robin had earned an enviable reputation as a resourceful sapper with a flair for achieving feats of engineering in record time. Thus the 200 or so men I took over were a hard-driving professional bunch with world-wide experience.

The unit was nicknamed 'the Beavers' because of its origins in Canada and the fact that this beast is the engineer of the animal world. Enemies hinted that, as this evil-tempered rodent spent its life messing up people's back gardens, eating forests, sleeping and mating, it was a good title for us!

Our first active service tour was in Ulster and it was amongst the green fields, leafy woods and dirty back streets of County Armagh that we sought the cold-blooded killers and their fiendish devices. Again I was lucky, because my immediate superiors were men who appreciated our dash and our unconventional methods. The brigade commander was Brigadier (now Major-General) Peter Bush, a tall, thin infantryman whom I knew well and liked immensely, whilst the Commander Royal Engineers was a charming colonel called John Yerburgh, who gave us every assistance and support to enable the hazardous work to be done efficiently. Few soldiers want war, but it is so much easier to achieve good results when under pressure if you haven't got to fight your superiors as well!

The squadron was certainly hard-pressed and although we had our successes there were casualties. By the time we returned to Ripon, the gallant sergeant major, WO 2 Ian Donald, had been killed, a sergeant working with us had also died and several men were wounded. However, there had still been moments of humour. One was the time we received a report of a woman acting suspiciously. She was seen to creep furtively out of her cottage at dawn and dusk and place something beneath an upturned bucket in her garden. The Beavers sent in a search party at first light and whilst the police tried to question the lady we examined the bucket. Fearing a booby-trap we evacuated the neighbourhood and, using a long line from behind a stone wall, pulled it over. A very old tortoise waddled out!

On another occasion we experimented with some captured home-made explosives.

'I don't think it's up to much,' the brigadier had said, 'but you might try out a little.'

Thus I piled it up in a remote car park two miles from Armagh. Over the radio I called the operations room of the resident battalion.

'I'm just going to set off a small, controlled explosion,' I warned the duty officer.

'Roger, out,' came back the disinterested reply.

I nodded to Sapper Murphy, who grinned evilly as he pressed the firing button. With a shattering roar the car park disappeared in a blinding flash and my teeth jarred with the blast!

'If that was your small, controlled explosion, Holdfast, please give us a little more warning when you're going to do a big one,' came the voice of the duty officer over the radio. 'The bloody ceiling's fallen in.'

The car park had ceased to exist and the detonation, having been heard thirty miles away, prompted two rival terrorist groups to claim responsibility!

For some time we had suspected that smuggled arms had been delivered to a lonely farm near our base. It was thought that the guns were being brought across the border in cattle trailers. One evening when such a vehicle was seen to arrive with its springs bent under a great load, an observation post noticed that there were no cattle inside. 'This is it,' I thought, and ordered the entire squadron to march through the night and surround the farm. By first light the men of the cordon had covered every exit and the search teams stood by with labradors, electronic gadgets and prodders.

Using a loud-hailer I called upon the occupants.

'We greatly regret the inconvenience, but this farm is surrounded and it is to be searched. You are to come out with your hands above your heads.'

The atmosphere was tense; only the dawn chorus of the birds broke the stillness of the summer morning. From the farm there was not the slightest reaction. I tried again. Still nothing! Two or three of the Beavers coughed and a lad from Hull said, 'Sure yer got right place, sir?'

'This is ridiculous,' I thought, and decided to try hammering on the front door. Pistol and loud-hailer in hand, I approached and, finding a bell, rang it. No response. So, raising the loud-hailer, I delivered my ultimatum once more. I'd just finished when the door opened gently to reveal a frail little old lady with grey hair dressed in a faded red dressing-gown.

'Oh, it's a lovely morning,' she said in her soft Irish voice. 'Won't you come in now and have a cup of tea?'

I tried to explain that I was not alone.

'That's quite all right,' she persisted. 'Bring your friends in too.'

'Madam,' I said, 'I have two hundred men surrounding this house.'

'Well, they'll have to share the cups then,' she smiled sweetly.

It took me five minutes to explain to her that we had to search the place.

'Oh well, if you must, you must,' she said, 'but you'll please be careful of me boyfriend upstairs.'

She busied herself with the tea-making as six hefty sappers dealt with her companion – a gentleman in his late seventies, who was in bed sleeping off a drop of the hard stuff. At this point chaos broke out. Our sniffer dog met the farm cat, which attacked it, driving the labrador into the chicken house. Hens flew in every direction, pursued by the soldiers. A large lance corporal searching the hay loft fell through the floor on to an enormous black sow, which bolted, squealing, into the cow-shed. The cows got out and thus dogs, cats, hens, pigs and cattle began to circumnavigate the buildings, pursued by yelling soldiers who thought the whole thing was a good laugh. Meanwhile the old soak was being carried downstairs by the search team whilst he waved a bottle of evil-smelling liquid and sang, 'The Sash my Father Wore'.

It really looked as if we'd made complete fools of ourselves when suddenly a false wall was discovered in the barn. Peering in through a bayonet hole we could see rows of packing cases.

'The guns, at last, a real find,' we all thought.

But, alas, it was only butter – tons of it, smuggled in from Eire in the cattle trailers! The police just laughed. 'Oh, butter smuggling's very common, don't you know, and we haven't really got time to worry about that,' they said. The Beavers spent the morning repairing the damage and drinking the dear old lady's tea. Then we went away with a case of butter that she kindly gave us!

Back at Ripon a few weeks later, we prepared for our next task; to support the new RAF Harrier force.

Screeching out of a muddy field with two tons of assorted weaponry slung beneath it the RAF Harrier jet looked a most impressive fighter. It had been invented by a Yorkshireman, John Fozard, who had designed the 'jump jet' to land and take off vertically, fly at supersonic speeds, stop dead in mid-air, reverse backwards and, if necessary, operate from front-line woodland. Thus it was that we had gone to Germany to support the Harrier force during a NATO evaluation exercise in the autumn of 1973. We got to the flat Sennelager training area well in advance of the Air Force. Our job was to build the field base so that the planes could be easily hidden and have the facilities for landing and take-off. Within twenty-four hours of arrival the Beavers had set up camouflaged hides for the jets and laid seventy-foot-square landing pads. Meanwhile our earth-moving plant had been used to smooth our farm fields and turn them into airstrips.

The idea was then for the RAF to fly the aircraft quickly into the base, get themselves hidden and camouflage the rest of their equipment. Whilst they were doing this we continued to build defences, get their armaments and bombs underground and improve the access roads.

On this exercise there were two Harrier squadrons which could be broken up into a number of sub-units. Each had its own fuel and defence capability with facilities for developing reconnaissance film. Once in their hides the Harriers simply awaited their targets. The aircraft could be used in many different ways and one important role was to knock out enemy armour with their anti-tank rockets. They could also carry ordinary bombs and, if necessary, be used in air-to-air combat. However, they preferred to use their manoeuvrability and vertical characteristics to avoid enemy aircraft. They seemed particularly good at close reconnaissance when fitted with a pod of six cameras attached to the belly. Using this device they could take many thousands of different photographs in one sortie! The resultant film was processed by a mobile photographic unit and could then be presented in three dimensions for area assessment.

Once our sapper work was done we were able to enjoy the show. The target was given to the crews and the speed with which they reacted was incredible. Within minutes of a pilot leaving his tent in full flying kit he was in the air ready to pounce. The great ten-ton monster weapon had roared into action and taxied out of its hide on its five wheels to the airstrip. Although the Harrier could lift off vertically, this was thirsty work, so a longer strip of about one hundred yards was used where possible, to help conserve fuel. For the spectators it was certainly jolly exciting to watch the jets accelerating down the makeshift runways and, with their gigantic thrust, hurling themselves into the air.

The stream of air being driven out of the jets' nozzles generates a temperature of 600°C and a thrust of some 21 000 pounds. The noise was ear-shattering, but the principle only too simple. Instead of directing a thrust out of the back to push the aircraft horizontally, the outlet nozzles are turned by the pilot towards the ground. The plane is then catapulted by the downward blast of air. The rushing air rips off the turf and scatters grass and mud, like sand from a blaster. As soon as it was airborne, the Harrier, like a huge lethal dart, rocketed through the air at a speed of over 600 miles per hour. We watched them climb to above 40 000 feet in under three minutes and then out-fly, out-turn and out-manoeuvre the conventional 'starfighter' jets of the West German Air Force that acted as the enemy for the exercise. The technical superiority of the Harrier was incredible. Here we soldiers could admire some of the old spirit of the RAF going back to days when Spitfires thundered off football pitches, piloted by men in leather jackets and school scarves. Indeed this *élan* seemed to be percolating back into the Harrier force. The exercise was going extremely well and we worked on by night alongside the RAF. There were the occasional sudden operational moves to cope with and the odd water point to be built to supply the force in the field, but we could never resist stopping to watch one of these massive hawks screeching in to hover above the fir forests and land on the metallic square strips that we had laid in clearings. Once on the ground the aircraft quickly taxied back into its hide and was hidden from sight once more.

Gordon Pickles, a friendly reporter from the *Yorkshire Evening Post*, had come over with us to cover the exercise. Gordon knew the Beavers from our days in Ulster and was a most likeable and talented young journalist. Tragically he was killed in a motor accident a few months afterwards.

Now preparations for the next big expedition were getting under way and every spare minute was spent in planning.

On arrival in Yorkshire Judith and I had bought Brook House. Built for the local master draper, the square Victorian house stood on the outskirts of the little market town of Thirsk. I fell in love with that place. It had big rooms, with high ceilings and a great covered yard in which all the junk I'd accumulated over the years could be stacked. In the bubbling stream at the end of the garden, Emma, Victoria and I built miniature dams and bridges, then blew them up with fireworks or shot them to bits with the air-rifle. We adored the Dales, and the ageing Kinder, our yellow labrador bitch, loved the shooting days. The venerable old gun-dog enjoyed amazing health in spite of her advancing years, but perhaps some of the credit was due to our famous vet. James Herriot is every bit as good a vet as he is an author.

Mr Gibson, our gardener, produced succulent asparagus and greens by the hundredweight. I endeavoured to keep fit by running for miles over the fields whilst dieting like mad to get my weight down. The house almost became an explorers' club, with many old chums and new friends congregating there to discuss, to argue, to devise and to plan for new ventures. Our good fairy was Mrs Armstrong who helped Judith to provide endless meals and cope with the constant stream of visitors. When things got a little hectic she'd chase us out with broad Yorkshire good-humoured scoldings of 'Aye, you're all mad.'

It was an exciting time from an exploration point of view and also from the military angle. I managed to get many trips overseas; in February 1974 the squadron sent a troop to Belize, another to Belfast and I took the rest of the unit to a country I had previously visited in 1966 – Oman.

4. The desert war

The desert sultanate lies in southern Arabia with its province, Dhofar, bordering on the Indian Ocean. This coastal territory separates South Yemen, better known as Aden, from the oil-rich Persian Gulf, where six giant tankers pass each hour through the narrow Straits of Hormuz carrying the precious life-blood for the West. Since the British withdrawal from Aden, the former colony has become a Marxist base and in 1974 was actively supporting a long-standing rebel war in Dhofar. The rebels' strategic aim was the Gulf; Soviet arms were sent in and local revolutionaries received training in China and Russia. The oppressive rule of Said bin Taimur, the aged sultan of Oman, complete with his long-standing alliance with the Imperial British and the poverty-stricken population of Dhofar, were just the right ingredients for communist propaganda. The People's Front for the Liberation of the Occupied Arabian Gulf (PFLOAG) had grown from various rebel groups and initially it made good progress. Against them stood the poorly equipped sultan's army, consisting of barely 1000 combatants, including a large number of Baluchi mercenaries and a few seconded British officers in command. Then in 1970 the situation changed.

It was a quiet July afternoon in Salalah; the still air in the yard of the sultan's palace was hot and humid. Unnoticed by the household slaves, the local *Wali*'s son, a handful of Omani Askers, plus an amusing soldier of fortune whom I shall call Mike, entered the labyrinth of passages that led to the private apartment of the charming old tyrant. At first they were unopposed but suddenly the royal bodyguard discovered the intruders. Shots rang out, ricocheting off the thick stone walls. Dashing through the dark corridors, Mike came to a heavy door, behind which he assumed lay the sultan's room. Flinging it open and yelling, 'Your Majesty', he found himself looking down the barrel of a tripod-mounted machine-gun with its owner in the act of pressing the trigger. 'Clackety-click' went the weapon as it failed to feed a round into the breech. 'Christ,' swore Mike and, dealing swiftly with the opposition, dashed on to the next room. The door was locked and the answer to his inquiry, 'Your Majesty?', was a burst of shots through the wooden panels. 'Oh bother,' said Mike (or words to that effect). He was just wondering what to do next when a shot was heard within the room, instantly followed by a shriek of pain. Bursting in, Mike found the sultan hopping around holding his foot! Whilst trying to reload his pistol the ruler had accidentally shot himself. Mike, who knew the sultan well, helped him to the courtyard where a Land-Rover rushed him to hospital. Within minutes it was all over. Said bin Taimur signed a letter of abdication in favour of his Sandhurst-trained son, Prince Qaboos, and an RAF aircraft flew him to Britain where he lived out his last few years in a private suite at the Dorchester.

The new sultan immediately set about strengthening his armed forces and turning the tide against the PFLOAG.

This was why the force from the 48th Field Squadron, Royal Engineers, underwent some pretty hard training on the North Yorkshire moors in December 1973.

In freezing blizzards we practised our sapper tasks and got fit. 'Just imagine it's sand, lads,' grinned Sergeant Major Cox as the Beavers stumbled about in the snow and cursed this new jaunt, which they were convinced 'bloody Blashford-Snell' had dreamed up to keep them away from the fleshpots of Ripon.

When Jack Walker, my energetic quartermaster, had loaded all our stores and equipment into a fleet of RAF transports, we left Britain, still in the grip of winter, for the arid province of Dhofar.

After flying high above the featureless desert of Arabia we stopped to refuel at the RAF base on the island of Masirah, just off the coast of Oman. The last leg of the journey was short and suddenly a hazy coastline loomed ahead. Miles and miles of sandy beaches stretched as far as the eye could see. Breaking waves rolled in from the deep green ocean to pound the shore, upon which we could make out the dun-coloured houses of Salalah. Roaring in low over the fertile gardens of the city, the Hercules wasted no time circling the airfield and so risking a burst of enemy fire. In seconds we were down and taxied quickly between a line of oil drums filled with sand to give protection against shrapnel. The men's eyes screwed up in the intense glare as we deplaned and felt the sun scorching our skin.

'It's getting hotter,' said the outgoing sapper squadron commander who met me and explained that, although the province was largely a wasteland with barren mountains and just an occasional oasis, the plains of Salalah are an exception. This is because from June to September the south-west monsoon blows in from the sea. Known as the *Khareef*, it produces clouds that precipitate water on to the Qara Hills, filling the rivers that flow on to the Salalah Plain, and giving rise to spectacular waterfalls and raging torrents. When this happens the desert blooms into stunted jungles, lakes and rolling downlands of lush grass.

The Dhofar Brigade whom we were to support was commanded by a tough, dynamic officer with a twinkling eye and a grand sense of humour. I counted myself fortunate to serve under a man like Brigadier Jack Fletcher. He briefed me in the small headquarters on the edge of Salalah airfield; his suntanned hand moving deliberately across the map.

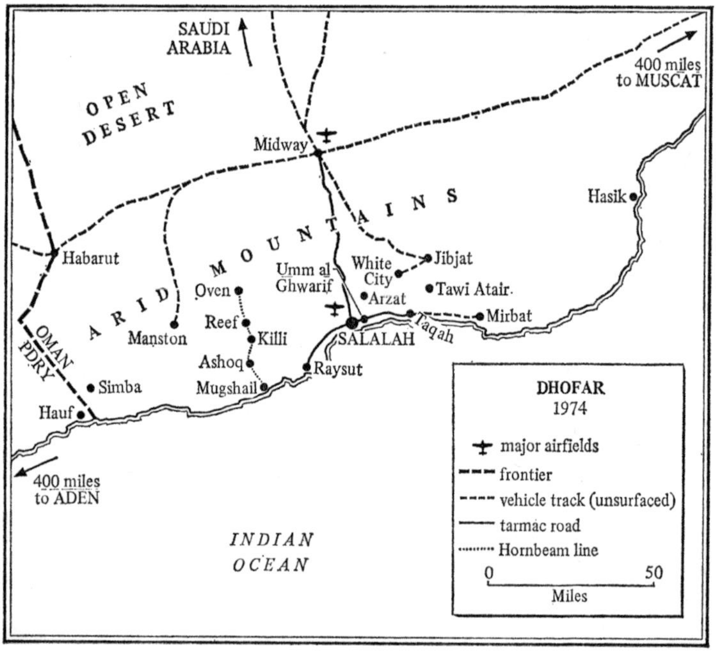

'In the eastern and central areas the Adoo have been driven back into the hills and now we must hunt them out. As we do this we need to convince the tribesmen that we are offering a better life than communism. So that's one of your jobs; to help us win over the hearts and minds of the people. But I also want you to give me the best sapper support you can to improve our defensive positions and living accommodation on the *jebel* before the wind and damp of the *Khareef* hits us in June.

'Then . . .' He paused to uncover a separate map and waited whilst the roar of a departing flight of Strike-masters subsided. The new map showed the mountains to the west.

'Now to where you can have a real field-day,' smiled Dynamite Jack, as he was known. 'The Hornbeam defensive line runs through these mountains. It's designed to stop enemy personnel and supplies getting to the eastern and central areas. We've started to wire it, but before the monsoon you must create the most deadly obstacle you can devise. The problem is that the line is thirty miles long. Wire is on its way, but mines are still in short supply. I can't spare many troops to help you and only helicopters can reach the hill-top positions. The Northern Frontier Regiment are holding the line with a battery of guns in support. I suggest you pop down and see Brian Ray* and then let me have your plan – in say two days' time. And, by the way, do you know anything about finding water?'

'I'm ready to try,' I replied.

'Good. Well, you'd better see what you can do for Simba.' He pointed out an isolated position where a battalion held a rocky bastion right on the frontier with South Yemen. They were completely surrounded, shelled and mortared daily, and relied entirely on helicopters to lift in their supplies of everything, including water.

In the outer office Peter Packham, the brigade major, offered his help. 'Anything you need, John, just ask me – we may not have it but at least we'll try to get it. And, by the way, are your chaps any good at concreting?' I added another little task to my growing list.

The next staff officer greeted me with a grin. 'I know all about you from my staff captain Q,' he said. Les Simcock, lately of the Parachute Regiment and now a captain in the sultan's armed forces, smiled up from his desk.

* Lt-Col. J. B. Ray MBE, the Queen's.

'Good heavens!' I exclaimed. 'Simcock, the butcher.' I had last seen him in Ethiopia in 1966 on one of the Sandhurst expeditions.

'We're here to help you, but you may be able to assist us,' he said. 'Can you build air-portable ration stores?'

In another room Wing Commander Ian Worby, commander of the sultan's air force, handed me a glass of iced lemonade and asked if we could construct landing pads for a new squadron of Wessex helicopters that were expected to arrive in ten days' time. I got back to my windowless office at Umm Al Gawaarif with enough work to keep an engineer regiment going for weeks, let alone a small squadron. Peter Page, my wiry, energetic second-in-command, whose immediate ambition was to get a place on the forthcoming Army Everest Expedition, cleared the layers of freshly blown sand from the operations room table and we sat down to study the map. As we worked on the deployment plan Jack Walker began to list all the nails, timber, sheets of 'wriggly tin',* explosive, cement, hand tools, barbed wire, mines and vehicles that we needed. In such an unsophisticated country as Oman the job of obtaining these items was no easy task. Everything was 'on order' or 'on the high seas somewhere' or would 'arrive tomorrow, *Insh'allah*'!†

On the rocky *jebel* even sand was in short supply, and if concrete was required in the defensive positions, we had to deliver cement, water and sand to the site by aircraft!

It was quite apparent that victory in this war depended just as much on the logistic back-up as on the skill and courage of the front-line troops. However, before we could serve effectively alongside the sultan's men we needed to acclimatize, and thus I planned a week's intensive training aimed at getting the Beavers used to working in the blistering heat and building up a protective tan on their skin. We did physical training on the beach, swam in the rushing surf and zeroed our weapons on a nearby range. Each day we exposed our bodies to the merciless sun for a little longer and rapidly the lily-white torsos turned a deep brown.

On the fourth day we mounted a simple operation with the aim of building a corrugated iron school at the coastal village of Hasik seventy miles east of Salalah.

* Corrugated iron.

† 'If God wills.'

The people, mainly fisherfolk, had been resettled on a flat plain separated from the Adoo and the rest of the Dhofar by the towering peaks of the *jebel*. Using a fleet of box-like Skyvan transport aircraft we moved men, tools, stores and water over the pale brown crags and canyons. The terrain was stark, awe-inspiring and frightening. Ranulph Fiennes,* who had served with distinction in the Muscat Regiment, had told me much of this desolate land where mere survival against the elements is a battle itself, without the added complication of the deadly human enemy.

Winging our way through the great gorges we rounded a bend to find the green ocean waiting. The mountains fell away in vertical buttresses as we dived steeply on to the short air-strip. Skyvan engines have an unusual characteristic of not changing pitch as they land and it was therefore comforting to realize that we were in fact slowing down.

Men and children poured out from the houses and shacks to meet us and, without bidding, began to cart all our equipment towards the school site. The area was peaceful and no Adoo had been seen there in recent times, so the work progressed rapidly. As the school went up, Sergeant Major Eddie McGee of the Army Physical Training Corps, who had come with me, put his knowledge of the area to good use. Chatting up the locals in a Yorkshire dialect of Arabic, he found that one youngster had fallen backwards on to a broken bottle, which had gone right up his rectum. When the sergeant major arrived he found the boy in a terrible state. The villagers, having no proper medical facilities, had covered the dreadful wound with camel dung, believing it to be antiseptic. Whilst this was going on the leader of these poor people thanked us for the school, presented me with a pair of ibex horns (to which putrefying meat still clung) and asked why we had not provided desks, chairs and a blackboard!

Leaving John Hoskinson, the sapper troop commander, to finish the job I flew back to Salalah, taking with me the prostrate bottle-squatter, from whom most of the manure had been removed, and also my rotting trophy. It was not the most pleasant of flights.

Being in an Arab country we worked normally on Sunday; Friday, or *Jummah*, is the day of rest. On the *jebel* we worked seven days a week, but when in Salalah the squadron usually

* Sir Ranulph Twistleton-Wykeham-Fiennes, Bt.

spent *Jummah* by the sea. White women were almost unknown in Dhofar and the Arab ladies lived in purdah, so relaxation was centred around fishing, swimming, boating, football, eating and drinking. The sea yielded up a fascinating array of fish. Spanish mackerel and crayfish became welcome additions to our menu and the cook sergeant, a massive jovial man, produced some mouth-watering dishes. Nevertheless caution was advisable when swimming because of the high population of potentially dangerous creatures. Helicoptering along the coast we could see giant Indian rorqual whales; over one hundred feet long, this dorsal-finned monster is the largest living animal. Lying close beneath the cliffs they blew spouts of water skyward and it was said that at night they uttered near-human cries. Saw-fish, stingrays, octopus, monster groupers and aggressive moray eels were frequently encountered, whilst the much-feared hammerhead sharks mingled with the playful and harmless dolphins amongst the inshore reefs. However, in spite of such a population of predators no one was attacked.

For my own part I should have loved to explore some of the archaeological sites of this ancient land. In fact only a few miles east of our base camp lay the ruins of Sumuran. The temple of the moon-god Sin had stood here in 1000 BC, guarding the stores of frankincense that were distributed by camel-train to every corner of Arabia and even to parts of the Roman Empire. Two thousand years ago it had been a great city and trade centre. But my real interest in the site was the result of my earlier exploration in Ethiopia. The Queen of Sheba, who plays such an important role in that country's history, is believed to have been Yemeni and it was she who exploited the use of frankincense from Sumuran as an international trading commodity and fixed great caravan routes with her northern ally and lover, King Solomon. Alas, there was no opportunity for an expedition and I simply made some notes for a visit at a future date.

As the monsoon approached, the ramshackle camp at Umm Al Gawaarif, with its limited air-conditioning, became a paradise and a cold beer a dream. In the relative cool of the evening we planned our operations, whilst out on the Salalah Plain the artillery thumped as the men of the outer defences engaged fleeting targets located on radar.

In the Muscat Regiment mess I was made most welcome and

often joined Mike, the soldier of fortune, for a glass of malt whisky and a chance to pick this highly experienced officer's brains. No one knew more about this complex campaign than he and no one else survived being blown up in a Land-Rover by a Russian anti-tank mine three times!

On one operation Mastodon, my faithful bulldozer, was to hit one such Soviet device whilst improving the road from the defended oasis of Jibjat, north of the desert town of Midway. By a miracle, and thanks to the steel anti-mine plates, the operator escaped unhurt. However, this represented 50 per cent of my dozer force so recovery and repair were essential.

Mines were an ever-present threat. Both British models left behind in Aden and modern Russian versions were present. However, some were buried too deeply to be effective and we surmised that this was done by a surrendering enemy who, after his conversion to the sultan's cause, could suddenly 'discover' the mine and claim the generous bounty offered! A favourite place for the dreaded PMN Russian anti-personnel mine to be placed was in an old sangar – a rock-walled defensive position. Sangars littered the province but you entered a long-disused one at your peril. Visiting a sapper in hospital one day I saw a Baluchi soldier brought in without legs, hands, face or sexual organs after stepping on one of these. Yet he lived!

By the middle of March our men had become experienced desert hands, bronzed and dusty, and they moved from one defensive locality to another providing essential engineer support. We seldom saw the elusive enemy, although undoubtedly they watched us and, when you least expected, there would be the crack of a high-velocity round or the crash of a mortar bomb. They were always 'out there somewhere' in the shimmering dun-coloured hills; usually only the eyes of the Firquat, the irregular troops of the sultan's army, many of them ex-Adoo and some with brothers still in the opposition, would pick out our hidden foes. We grew to rely on the Firquat to warn us of an enemy presence, but even they slipped up sometimes, as one of our sections discovered.

A ramp down a steep escarpment was being built by the faithful bulldozers, assisted with liberal quantities of plastic explosive, when an aged and rather dusty tribesman approached some sappers. He jabbered away in Jebali and when our lads shook their heads and said, 'Sorry, Johnnie, don't speak the lingo', he became most excited and appeared to be pleading with them. 'No, Buckshesh, now go on, push off, will you,' they retorted. Thus the poor fellow went from group to group without success. Eventually he found an Omani NCO of the escorting infantry platoon who certainly did react. The man was an Adoo trying to get someone to accept his surrender!

Relations with the Firquat were never easy. Proud men and traditional fighters, they had few material possessions, but believed it their right to have everything provided for them. They seldom carried any water of their own and on operations they would often demand that the sultan's regular soldiers should give them some. If this was refused they would sulk and become childish, saying, 'You do not like us, you will not give us water, see, you are not our brothers after all.' The *jundee** who had carried his precious water for miles could hardly be expected to sympathize. Of us the Firquat demanded 'wriggly tin' and building materials for their houses and even the use of bulldozers to improve their villages! Yet they fought well and had to be encouraged. This difficult task fell to the highly professional bunch of experienced regular soldiers, known as the British Army Training Team. Their courage and skill were legendary, as was their patience in handling these irregulars.

I often met the Firquat at the defended oasis named Tawi Atair. As was the case with most such areas, the occupation depended on a water source, but Tawi Atair was unique in that the precious liquid was brought up from an underground lake at the bottom of a massive sink-hole.

One of the first tasks of the Royal Engineers in Dhofar had been to install a submersible pump to raise the water up an iron pipe and thus fill drinking troughs for the people's livestock. This had been done before our squadron had arrived but, because the pump required maintenance, we grew to know the site rather well.

Access to the caverns was gained by first descending some 300 feet into a huge cavity of rectangular cross-section with the long axis running approximately east–west. Then there followed a hair-raising journey down a 270-foot vertical pipe which our predecessors had installed, welding on bars to act as steps or rungs at intervals. Peter Page's mountaineering expertise was extremely valuable at Tawi Atair.

* A regular soldier in the sultan's army.

Descending into the hole, we could see a number of old, dry water-beds running down the sides. Finally at the base of the shaft there were many entrances to cave systems, some of which led into huge underground lakes. Our divers had explored one of these and found water depths down to 110 feet. Small, almost translucent fish, which I imagined to be blind, were seen swimming at various levels. These creatures were losing their skin pigmentation, which was basically white but with a very pale pink band around the gill area. With our chums at the British Museum in mind I tried to get some captured alive but we failed miserably. They might be blind but they always managed to elude our divers.

From the amount of driftwood discovered in the cavern, it would appear that at the time of the rare heavy rains the whole shaft must fill up to a level of approximately sixty feet above that which we saw. Running water could be heard falling within the caverns and we decided that even if we installed a second pump there was little danger of running the incredible source dry. At this time there was only one pump in position and, if it failed, the numerous cattle, goats and camels that relied upon it would die. So it was that the sappers set to and installed a reserve. Watched by curious weaver birds who nested inside the rim we lowered our paraphernalia down into the depths to complete the task. The worst part of the whole operation was climbing back up the iron pipe to the surface. One rung was missing at the precise point where one had to negotiate an overhang. Unfortunately we had neither the time nor the equipment to make a complete exploration of this fascinating cavern system; but perhaps that may be done by another expedition.

Throughout Dhofar water is the key to life. North of the *jebel* lay the greatest sand desert in the world – the Rubh Al Khali, or 'Empty Quarter'. It stretches for 1000 miles from the coast of Oman island to Saudi Arabia. In this harsh region lived the nomadic Bedu whose main interests were camels and simply keeping alive.

Patrick Brook's armoured cars prevented the enemy from crossing this enormous obstacle and reaching the *jebel* from the north. The sultan's army also maintained one or two small defensive positions from which Patrick could operate, and the main job for our squadron in this area was to find water and build wells. Normally one was not disturbed by the enemy but on one occasion a section of sappers had been dismayed to discover that the aircraft they had been watching approach was not a supply plane bringing mail and rations but an Ilyushin bomber. They took cover in their well and luckily the bombs fell wide. Back at home things were none too peaceful either and shortly after we arrived in Oman we learned that the IRA had bombed our camp in Yorkshire! The one good thing that came out of that was that we managed to get the whole place redecorated far more quickly than we should otherwise have done.

Our priority task was the improvement of the Hornbeam line. On my reconnaissance visit I was greatly impressed with this amazing terrain. Deep wadis separated the waterless mountain tops on which the soldiers of the Northern Frontier Regiment lived in underground bunkers. Having drawn up a plan with Brian Ray and received the brigadier's blessing we set to work. Firstly we had to complete the wiring and then thicken up the mine fields in between the infantry company positions. Thus I moved my tactical headquarters to a heavily blasted hill top named Ashoq. The summit of this mountain was occupied by B Company under a delightful Scotsman named Angus Ramsay. His second-in-command was Charlie Daniel, a Royal Marine who, with half the company and the mortars, held the end of a long ridge that stretched north for several miles from Ashoq. Standing on Angus's hill-top we could look south to the Indian Ocean and north to the skyline beyond which the Hornbeam line ended.

When I had helicoptered into Ashoq I had noticed how white the summit appeared. On close inspection I discovered this was due to the enormous number of direct hits it had received from Soviet Katyusha 122 mm missiles fired from as far away as seven miles by the Adoo. Angus kept a small museum of the remains of these onslaughts and an area of ground outside his command post was covered with rows of tail fins, shell splinters and shrapnel that he had picked up in the relatively short time he'd been there. A direct hit by a Katyusha could knock a rock-built sangar clean off the hill. To reduce this hazard we were able to assist the infantry by using our electrically driven Hi-cycle drills to bore down into the soft rock and blast out deeper bunkers for them.

The Katyushas could usually be heard approaching and a lookout would shout 'incomer' on his personal VHF radio.

All officers and NCOs carried these small radios and, as soon as the words were broadcast, all would dive for cover. With luck you might have four seconds to do this; it seemed extraordinary to me, when considering how many rockets had landed on this position, that there had never been a single fatal casualty caused by them. Most injuries were due to people banging their heads and shins as they jumped into the holes. However the enemy rocket crews did suffer (as we learned from Radio Aden), when the Strike-masters bombed the dust-cloud caused by the Katyusha's firing.

The Adoo were only about 1400 yards away across the far side of a deep valley. At night their radio conversations could be heard quite clearly on our own sets and Ashoq frequently received mortar bombs and recoiless rifle shells in addition to the missiles.*

My first night with Angus was an alarming one. He kindly produced a large bottle of Scotch which flowed freely while he briefed me on the situation. There was little room inside the rock-walled command post but I was quite comfortable on the floor. The first interruption of my night's sleep was the feeling that something smooth and warm was sliding over me. It was: a small grey sand viper. A few moments later a rat with Mickey Mouse ears bounded over my legs chasing the snake and then came fleeing back in the other direction as the viper pursued the rat. Relaxation was not easy under these conditions, but I had just dropped off when there was the most ear-shattering noise. I realized at once that the heavy machine-gun in the next bunker had opened up. Forgetting rats and snakes I rushed out to see what was happening, only to hear Angus groan from his pit, 'Bet you it's foxes they're shooting at.' Outside, in the delightful cool of the night, I could see flares alight in the mine field and watched the tracer curving away into the distance. Eventually a somewhat sleepy Angus emerged to see what was going on. But he need not have worried because one of the Arab officers had the situation perfectly under control and after ten minutes of fireworks we returned to bed. An hour later the same thing happened again; this time Angus was a little concerned that it might be an attempted intrusion through

* On average there were twenty mortar bombs or recoiless rifle shells per week and ten Katyushas per month. The Katyushas were probably limited by the logistic problem of carrying the 120-pound rockets over the difficult terrain.

the line and so some mortar fire was put down to deter anyone lurking out there.

The sapper is a very adaptable chap and soon our men were completely integrated with their Arab hosts. Living and eating with them presented no problems although at best our men could speak only a little Arabic and few of the Arabs knew even one word of English.

The mine-laying was not made any easier by the presence of a large number of unmarked mines that had been laid by previous occupants. I soon discovered that the planning figures so religiously stated in our manuals do not apply when you are dealing with live mines. I would recommend multiplying the theoretical timings by five if you are to get the right number of mines per man laid by soldiers who have only used plastic or concrete ones previously. One of Charlie Daniel's NCOs accidentally tripped one of our little toys during a skirmish. It was a fiendish device which, when activated, would jump into the air and explode at shoulder height, throwing shrapnel all around it for distances up to one hundred yards. Known as 'jumping jacks', these were amongst the most deadly mines we possessed. However Charlie and his NCO were extremely lucky and got away with minor scratches, but from then on people treated our mine fields with a very great respect.

A gruesome relic of an earlier attempt by the enemy to get through the line could be seen quite clearly across the far side of a deep wadi. If you looked through binoculars you could make out the whitening bones of a skeleton, without a head. Known to the soldiers as Jonah, this unfortunate fellow had been killed by one of the 'jumping jacks' a few months before. Charlie had gone out to investigate and while approaching, heard some noise and took cover. A few moments later he was able to witness the awful scene when a small pack of Arabian red wolves came stealthily down the track, avoided the other mines with great care and then feasted on the corpse. Although some valuable papers and documents were recovered after this incident it was not possible to get the body out without risking life and limb by going into the mine field, and therefore Angus decided to leave it. This greatly upset our own Arab soldiers who believed that, although a communist, the man must still be a true believer and should be brought back and given the appropriate burial.

Sappers of the 48th Field Squadron RE race for cover after being helicoptered on to the Hornbeam line in Dhofar

Wessex helicopter of the Sultan's air force lifts sappers from their minefield during operations on the Hornbeam line, Dhofar 1974. Enemy were on the ridge in the background

Angus Ramsay (*left*) and Mike Bourne of the Northern Frontier Regiment with captured Adoo weapons and souvenirs of the bombardment of Ashoq – 122mm Katyuska missiles, 75mm RCL and mortar bombs

One of Patrick Brook's splendid Saladin armoured cars that often escorted the Royal Engineers in Dhofar

The great sink hole at Tawi Atair, Dhofar. Royal Engineers installed submersible pumps at the bottom to bring water and thus life to the desert at the top

Sappers of the 48th Field Squadron RE clearing mines in Dhofar

Johnnie Braddell-Smith (right) by his Company HQ on the Hornbeam line

I have always enjoyed working with Arabs and I found the Omanis to be no exception. They were interesting people and some of their strange ways were fascinating. One soldier of B Company who was said to possess special powers could take a poisonous sand viper and place its head inside his mouth and then close his lips around the neck with no apparent ill effects. However, I noticed that before he did this he put a spell, or *hesp*, on the creature.

Once the work on the line was going well I moved forward to the isolated position known as Simba. The cool early morning air left us shivering as we boarded the Iranian helicopter to fly forward. Packed in with us were some 400 pounds of explosive, two 'burmils'* of water and three sacks of rather smelly goat meat. The flight over the sea was as beautiful as ever and it was only a short while before we were touching down at a camp called Manston to dump off part of our load. The Iranian pilot gave me a toothy grin and a thumbs-up sign as we took off on the last leg of our journey. Now I was the only passenger and the meat had been replaced with more water. Beneath us there were deep shadows in the steep-sided wadis and the stark dry hills stood out clearly in the first rays of the morning sun. Not speaking Persian, I couldn't understand the pilot's conversation with ground control but he did look rather agitated. Glancing up I was just in time to see two Strike-masters diving steeply past us towards the ground.

Far below I could just make out the defensive positions and see the narrow scar that I knew must be the airstrip. The runway was clear, but amongst the broken ground on either side lay the wreckage of several aircraft. Enemy fire had prevented the use of fixed-wing planes to land stores and so now all supplies came in by helicopter. I had lost sight of the Strike-masters when something attracted my attention. I saw two white streamers heading groundward and realized that they were rockets that had just been fired from the leading fighter. The flash of the explosion followed almost at once and then I saw the other plane release its rockets before pulling up once again. Now we could see small puffs of smoke drifting about in a haphazard way on the position and I realized that we were flying into the middle of a bombardment.

Our pilot was clearly in two minds about landing, but I gesticulated wildly, pointing at my load of explosive and the

* Forty-gallon oil drums, a corruption of Burmah oil.

water, both of which were important for the defence of the garrison. The Iranian smiled again, this time a little nervously, and took us down in a tight spiral towards the landing pad. As we neared the ground the puffs of grey smoke got bigger. Our shadow raced up to meet us and the skids were barely on the rock when a Baluchi sergeant came running forward to help me lift down our lethal cargo.

As I jumped out he said in English, 'Good morning, sahib,' and saluted! 'I have a Land-Rover right here,' he added as we dragged the stores away from the helicopter, whilst the pilot yelled at us to hurry up. As the last box was removed, the Huey rose in a cloud of dust and whirled skyward again. Now that we were no longer deafened by the engine noise, the crash of the mortar bombs and the thump of the guns was clearly audible. No time was wasted in loading the battered Land-Rover, and then, with the Baluchi at the wheel, we took off at a frightening pace down a bumpy track towards battalion headquarters. On arrival he insisted on jumping out and opening the door, and saluted once again. An explosion sounded very close and I was glad to dive into the cool darkness of the command post. Making my way through the labyrinth of sandbag walls, I came to the open-topped observation post where a British officer was controlling the jets, guns, mortars and everything else by radio.

'Good morning,' he said with a smile. 'I'm rather busy at the moment – would you excuse me for a few minutes?'

I sat down on an aircraft seat that had clearly been dragged from the wreckage of one of the planes I had seen lying beside the runway. There was a murmur at my elbow and I looked up to see, to my surprise, a mess orderly in a white jacket holding a silver tray on which stood spotlessly clean cups and saucers and a pot of coffee.

'Coffee, sahib,' he smiled.

A few minutes later the battle had ended.

'Well, that's this morning's show over,' sighed the acting battalion commander as he joined me for coffee. 'So you think you may be able to find some water for us.'

'I'll certainly try,' I replied.

'Good. Well, I've got a section of men who will go with you. Better have a long drink first though; it's quite a way and a good climb. And, by the way, be a bit careful – we've mined the wadi bed.'

Thus it was that, within the hour, our small party of engineers was stepping warily over the trip wires, seeking any patch of greenery or damp sand which might indicate the presence of water. I was just examining a likely spot when there was a loud 'pop' behind me. Certain it was one of the wretched 'jumping jacks', I hurled myself flat. The Baluchi soldiers roared with laughter. It had only been a trip flare!

Having selected one or two possible sites where water might be found if the sappers dug deep enough, I returned to battalion headquarters and flew back to Salalah. On our flight from Simba we passed over an armed dhow of the sultan's navy. The crew waved from the deck as the helicopter zoomed homeward. These ungainly looking craft were far more effective than they appeared. They carried recoiless guns on deck and at night would creep in under the communist guns, unseen on the darkened sea. By using their machine-guns they would draw retaliatory fire from the Adoo; immediately an enemy weapon was pinpointed, the giant recoiless rifle would be brought to bear and send its heavy shell whistling shoreward. The back-blast was enormous and, as soon as it had fired, the dhow would make out to sea with all speed, usually followed by heavy mortaring from the shore.

Back on the Hornbeam line, Angus and Charlie were still at work harassing the enemy with daring patrols that would lay mines and booby-traps along the supply routes, deep inside Adoo territory. Sometimes these devices were discovered by enemy sappers and detonated or, worse, used against us.

It was 1130 hours on a June morning when a mine was seen to explode in front of Ashoq. Immediately Angus used the battalion's supporting artillery to shell the area and then flew forward in a helicopter to direct a strike by the jet fighters on to the area. Although he was unable to see any sign of movement on the ground, he decided that a rapid follow-up was justified in the hope of finding enemy who might have been wounded by mines, artillery or the air attack. Accordingly he arranged to sally forth that afternoon, provided that the cloud was sufficient to cover his approach.

At 1700 hours the swirling mists were low on Ashoq, with visibility being about 200 yards. Then Angus decided to move in daylight and trust to the cloud for cover, as it was imperative that he could see the mined area in daylight. So fifteen minutes later he left his position with a thirty-strong patrol, including

Charlie and Lieutenant Salim Said. They moved west without incident until they reached a track junction. Like all experienced infantry commanders Angus had arranged for fire to be available on call from the guns supporting the battalion. Therefore, as he continued to advance, artillery fire was put down to clear the route ahead. At the track junction he arranged his forces in all-round defence, with four picket positions on the higher ground and his headquarters in the centre. Then he went forward to investigate the mines. Two locations were untouched, but in a third, a mine had been pulled by the enemy using a long length of string which was still in position. This was the mine that had been seen to explode.

Angus now sent Charlie plus Staff Sergeant Ali Salin and Lieutenant Salim Said, with an escort of three soldiers to check out the wadi-head south of the track, whilst he himself examined the wadi-head north of the track with a similar escort. Both areas showed evidence of having been well strafed by the fighters.

Without warning at 1845 hours a salvo of twenty-five-pounder shells landed with thunderous noise 200 yards south of Angus's position. Unable to understand what had prompted this he ran to his radio operator, gave the order, 'Check firing', and asked the artillery what the devil they were up to. The gunner was explaining when small-arms fire broke out in the south and a violent battle began.

Charlie and his group had moved down their wadi to the south approximately 150 yards, having left three soldiers to picket the high ground on the east. Rounding a bend, Charlie had bumped into seven enemy moving out of the mist towards him at only twenty-five yards' range. One of them was a woman. They were in single file with their Russian weapons slung over their shoulders. A further group could be heard, out of sight, in the rear. Charlie's party turned and ran like stags back up the wadi. They split up after twenty-five yards, Charlie running on up the wadi whilst Salim Said and the staff sergeant ran to the picket position. The enemy reacted at once and came after them in hot pursuit, firing from the waist with their Kalashnikov AK47 automatic rifles. Bullets slammed into the ground all around him as Charlie went faster and faster along the track. He had never run so fast in his life.

On hearing the gunfire, Angus had moved forward with a

sergeant for about twenty-five yards down the wadi, when he saw Charlie coming like a rocket towards him. He almost seemed to disappear in clouds of dust as the bullets struck about him. Barely fifty yards behind came the enemy spread out across the valley. Angus slammed his rifle into the aim, fired, and sent one of the Adoo somersaulting backwards. However, a companion picked him up and all four took cover behind some rocks. Angus continued to blaze away at them as they disappeared in the swirling mist. By now Charlie had reached him, panting furiously, and as he did so they were again engaged, this time by three enemy from high ground to the east. This came as a nasty shock because Angus believed his own picket to be up there.

Meanwhile Salim Said and the staff sergeant had also managed to make their way back under heavy fire. But Angus was still wondering what on earth had happened to his picket as the firing became heavier. Then one of his mortar men was hit in the leg and so Sergeant Saif Salim took over the 60 mm mortar and began to return the fire. However, they were too close for this high-trajectory weapon to be truly effective and Angus, realizing that the three men he had been looking at on the picket position were in fact enemy, quickly shot the centre one in the stomach. The man collapsed and a second later Charlie hit the right-hand Adoo, whilst the staff sergeant got the last one as he was running away.

However, they had no time to congratulate themselves, for by now the remaining enemy, who had originally been chasing Charlie, had gained the high ground to the west and their fire was beginning to inflict casualties. A corporal who was standing up and shooting at them was hit in the head and killed outright. Crawling over to the prostrate NCO, Angus checked his pulse because he seemed to be moving, but alas it was only the nervous system reacting: he was very dead. But now all B Company patrol were returning the fire against the three enemy in the west and eventually silenced them. For a moment there was quiet. Then shooting broke out again from the west, but it was coming from dead ground, so Angus called for artillery support. Unfortunately he was now out of range of the guns in the centre of the Hornbeam line and there was some delay whilst the fire mission was passed through to the southern battery near battalion headquarters. However, in spite of great difficulties with communications, the message got through and after several minutes shells came screaming down on the rear of the enemy position.

Meanwhile B Company's western pickets, which consisted of two groups of six men each with a general purpose machine-gun, were being heavily engaged by up to forty enemy who were attacking out of the monsoon clouds. The Adoo quickly drove the pickets to take cover in some nearby caves whilst Staff Sergeant Imam Bux took over a machine-gun and held the enemy off. However, one of Imam Bux's soldiers was badly wounded in the leg and once again they were forced to pull back.

Angus now gave the order by radio to his forces to withdraw east. So Staff Sergeant Imam Bux picked up the wounded man, the machine-gun and his own rifle and, covered by the other section, managed to get to dead ground in rear. This section then followed and in the depression Imam Bux reorganized them on the track and prepared to carry the wounded man eastwards towards Ashoq.

Meanwhile, during a lull in the firing, the headquarters group had moved on to the track and over it to the north. Charlie Daniel was organizing carrying parties and the Omani lieutenant, Salim Said, collected the dead corporal. Communications were hopeless. In dead ground Angus was screened from the artillery and it was proving impossible to get successful fire missions. By now darkness had fallen and Salim Said's party carried the corporal's body east, to where Charlie was organizing the comparatively uninvolved members of another picketing group and such men as were coming in.

At this stage, B Company had suffered one dead and five wounded. Angus and his signaller remained in position to cover the withdrawal of the gallant staff sergeant, Imam Bux, and his group who were carrying their wounded man. As this group passed Angus, the enemy gained the high ground on the west and very heavy fire was brought down. Three or four RPG7 rockets exploded in the wadi-head where the headquarters position had been only a moment before and another seven enemy began to fire on them with automatic rifles and machine-guns. Realizing the difficulty Angus was now in, Imam Bux engaged the Adoo with his own machine-gun at a range of only sixty yards and this caused the enemy fire to lift briefly.

Angus continued to call for support from the artillery, which only attracted the enemy who were now firing at his 'voice'. His signaller was shot in the face and knocked unconscious, so Angus grabbed the radio from the bleeding soldier and carried it himself. They were now both pinned down and unable to move, but the signaller was still alive. At this stage the nearest Adoo were about seventy yards away. Unable to see Angus, his own troops could no longer give effective covering fire from their positions to the rear. Campoda* Rasul Bux saw his commander's critical situation and came to help. Together they dragged the wounded signaller away. They were just in time, for as they left the prearranged artillery fire landed slap on the position, silencing the approaching enemy.

Moving over the rocky ground in the darkness, Charlie and Salim Said organized the move of the dead and wounded along the track to the east. The work was terribly exhausting; anyone who has ever carried a wounded man or a body knows it is no easy matter to withdraw in the teeth of the enemy for some 1500 yards, while carrying casualties. Angus acted as rear guard with three soldiers, continually calling down artillery fire on each vacated position to discourage pursuit. At last he managed to establish good communications and arrange for a helicopter to come in and pick up the dead and wounded. At the same time he called for his sergeant major and a section to come forward in the battered old Land-Rover that was kept at Ashoq to help them with the casualties. As the thick mist rolled over the *jebel*, a Wessex of the sultan's air force was guided in by a Sarbe radio and the lights of the Land-Rover. Thus ended a battle typical of many that were fought in this campaign.

There is no doubt about it, that working in the Scotch mist conditions of the *Khareef* was one of the most eerie sensations I've ever had to endure. It is quite different to that of being in complete darkness; somehow one felt that you were always being watched by unseen eyes peering through the drifting clouds.

Just north of Charlie Daniel's position was an enormous wadi called Jizalawt. It was a huge cleft in the mountains, over 2000 feet deep, and in the early days we suffered a number of casualties due to heat exhaustion from men simply trying to walk up and down the canyon. John Hoskinson, one of my troop commanders, had done sterling work in mining this

* The name given to all medical orderlies in the sultan's army.

natural route through the line. He was operating from the other side of the wadi with Staff Sergeant Yeomans and thirty of the toughest sappers you can imagine. Meanwhile I continued to work on the south side, seeding the mine field with a few specials that were designed to be set off electrically from an observation post on the rim of the canyon. It was now a race against time. The monsoon had started a little early and our task was not yet complete. Thus we could not afford to stop for weather conditions.

On one particular day I found myself halfway down the wadi side with a small party of sappers and Omanis when the clouds rolled in, reducing visibility to fifty yards. The temperature seemed to drop and I felt a shudder go down my spine. But an even bigger one came a moment later when I heard the familiar 'crump–crash' of mortars. The first bomb landed a few hundred yards away down the slope, chippings and splinters showered around us. I grabbed my walkie-talkie, but couldn't get through as we were shielded from our friends by the wadi rim. To try to climb up the way we had come down was now almost impossible. The rocks, dampened by the mist, were like a skid-pan and one risked falling hundreds of feet if one made a slip. Quickly we concealed the rest of our devices under the rocks and, getting the party together, tried to climb out, but for every pace we went forward we slid two backwards. There was only one thing to do: we tore up our shirts and, wrapping strips of cloth around our hands, began to pull ourselves up the barbed-wire fence that marked the mine field and led out of the valley. It was long, hard, nerve-racking business with the mortar bombs raining down from above. Each time one heard the noise of the descent one wondered where it was going to land. However, we eventually reached the top, where Salim Said greeted me. The explanation was quite simple. They had been his mortars; a sentry on top of the mountain had seen some enemy moving into the wadi below us. We had very sore hands but were extremely thankful.

I rapidly learned to admire the professionalism of the officers in the sultan's armed forces. Although we saw rather a lot of B Company, the Northern Frontier Regiment, their neighbours, A Company, were also good friends. When we had first started on the line the second-in-command, Ian Gardiner, a rugged marine, had been responsible for our escorts and safety and later I had many dealings with his commander,

Johnnie Braddell-Smith, one of the company commanders on the Hornbeam, who had advised me on the siting of the mines in the most likely places where they could catch penetrating parties of enemy.

Johnnie was a highly respected officer, beloved by his men, with a quiet manner that gave no indication of the fire that burned within him. He was a thoughtful, devoted and tolerant person under whom it was a pleasure to serve. His knowledge and interest in the Omanis was outstanding and in Salalah, while other officers might relax in their rooms taking refuge from the afternoon sun, it was frequently John's pleasure to go out around the barrack blocks, talking and eating with the soldiers. As a result, he built up an impressive store of knowledge about the individuals in his company, their families, their homes, their fears and their aspirations. This deep interest in the well-being of his men, together with his wisdom and skill as a commander, inspired a loyalty and affection such as are rarely seen in a military environment. His outstanding characteristic was his unflappability, which must have contributed greatly towards his bravery. But it was his ability to take the sting out of even the most formidable situations that will be remembered most. There were many instances of this, but one of the most notable was an action that took place in the Wadi Sha'ath.

Intelligence had indicated that there might be a party of some sixteen enemy based in the area immediately to the east of the Hornbeam line, where they were acting as a reception committee for those Adoo who succeeded in getting through our defences. Accordingly A Company mounted an operation to hunt them out. Thus four platoons, supported by mortars, moved into the area and laid night ambushes. The following morning Johnnie sent Ian and two of the platoons further east to take up new positions, while he remained in ambush with the rest. At 1130 hours, about ten Adoo appeared and were in the act of walking into Johnnie's killing ground when Ian's half of the company came under heavy and accurate fire further east. On hearing the shooting the ten enemy took cover and thus avoided being caught in Johnnie's ambush. Meanwhile his second-in-command's forward platoon had taken up a position on a small *jebel* to the south of their initial position. Ian was moving with the rear platoon on ground which was not to his advantage and he started taking casualties straight away. The soldier on the general purpose machine-gun was killed almost immediately and, of the party of four who came to assist with the dead man, another was wounded and one killed. In the face of such a heavy attack Ian's group was forced to withdraw in a hurry, leaving bodies and equipment in open ground. They consolidated their position as best they could with the remainder of the platoon, and Ian now called to Johnnie for help.

He had no idea how many enemy there were. To begin with, probably not very many, but it soon became apparent that there were considerably more than the sixteen with whom they had originally come to do battle. In fact, intelligence subsequently indicated that up to sixty Adoo had passed through the Hornbeam line very recently. Ian's forward platoon was not in a position to afford direct assistance and they were having troubles of their own anyway. To make matters worse communications had broken down. The intensity of the fire steadily increased, despite sterling work by the mortars and jets that had now come up to support A Company. Nothing could be done to prevent the enemy flanking movements or their attempts to loot the bodies. A Company were extremely keen to prevent looting and the loss of one machine-gun with 500 rounds of ammunition as well as a radio set would not have been to their credit. Although the Adoo did approach the bodies and took a rifle it was curious to note that they seemed more interested in the boots and *shemaghs* rather than the more war-like hardware. They also removed a dead Omani corporal's epaulets which had holes for badges of rank in them. Presumably they thought that they had killed an officer. By 1400 hours the battle was going very badly for A Company and they were in the depths of gloom and despair. Now low in ammunition, they were being out-flanked by the enemy and had sustained a further wounded casualty. Ian Gardiner admits that in all truth he had run out of ideas. If Johnnie did not arrive soon he could be of little use to them. But he did arrive. Ian was in a state of great agitation and exhorted him to position his troops as soon as he could. Diving for cover behind a rock, Johnnie sat recovering his breath and offered his second-in-command a drink of water. 'Look,' Ian said, frantically explaining the situation to him. Johnnie fumbled in his pocket and produced a crumpled packet of Rothmans and asked for a light. So they lay there, the pair of them, without saying a word, and smoked a cigarette while the enemy bullets zipped over their heads. Ian knew that everything was going to be all right.

The combined force now got themselves into a position where they could at least cover their casualties. Johnnie then organized a small party and, under cover of a jet strike, led them out to a hollow near where the dead men lay. Then on the next jet run, the Omani soldiers ran to the bodies, dashed round them and back again! Patiently Johnnie had another word with the men, led them out again and brought one body back. All this time they were being shot at by the Adoo. However, A Company's superior firepower was now beginning to have a satisfactory effect. Ian felt that it was his turn next, that he couldn't leave Johnnie to do all the work, so he rushed out and recovered a second body with the help of another party of four men. Meanwhile Johnnie sprinted out again and, darting around the battleground, recovered both the machine-gun and the radio set. By now A Company had the upper hand but there were at least two enemy trying to kill Johnnie while he achieved this feat.

Perhaps one may be forgiven for believing that to risk life for such a comparatively worthless end is completely nonsensical. Indeed, looking back now, Ian admits that his spine shivers. But, as he explains, it must be remembered that they had been told to recover the radio if at all possible and the Northern Frontier Regiment had never left a body for the enemy. To be the first to do so was unthinkable. Apart from anything else, they could never be sure that their friends were dead and the possibility that they might be left alive to be captured by the Adoo was a sufficient stimulus to drive everyone to almost any folly to prevent it.

Not everyone loved John Braddell-Smith. He was no respecter of persons and had an individual approach to things which did not always coincide with the ideals of his superiors; his performance at parties, with a few whiskies inside him, could be somewhat unconventional. He came from a happy, loving family in the south of Ireland and his chums found him a slightly introverted, compassionate, warm and human friend, although it was easy to see why he was not particularly happy living within the regimentation of the British Army.

In my last week in the mountains I spent a night with Johnnie sharing a bottle of Scotch and talking about Britain, the war and everything else that came to mind. Little did I know that I should never see him again. After I had left Oman the long-awaited advance took place. The sultan's army, reinforced with units of the Imperial Iranian Army, swept forward from the Hornbeam line to destroy the enemy and drive the survivors back to South Yemen. The fighting was bitter and there were many casualties. As I might have expected, in the forefront of it all was Johnnie.

He was now commanding a group of irregulars, the Firquat Tariq Bin Zaid, working with an Iranian task force. On 10 December 1974 an operation was mounted by an Iranian battalion to establish a position about a mile to the south of their main forward base, which was then on the edge of the tree-line. Johnnie led the advance through the trees at the front of one of the two columns of Iranian troops with complete disregard for his own personal safety. On reaching the objective he discovered that the main body had somehow become separated from him and so he immediately returned along his route and successfully made contact with the missing troops.

Later that day the Adoo attacked the position with heavy small-arms fire and RPG7 rockets which killed ten Iranian soldiers and wounded another. As soon as there was sufficient fire being directed against the enemy, Johnnie went forward to check the position. Moving stealthily around the company perimeter, he recovered the bodies of three Iranians who were thought to have been captured by the enemy. Those who watched him operate and organize the evacuation of casualties were greatly inspired by his personal example and tireless vigilance, which eventually enabled the company to withdraw without further losses, in spite of determined enemy attacks.

The next day the Iranian battalion sustained several more casualties in their forward locations. Because of the proximity of the Adoo it was not possible to evacuate the dead and wounded by helicopter and so the indefatigable Johnnie volunteered to take a Land-Rover forward from the main position, a distance of a couple of miles along an undefended route, with darkness falling rapidly. This action enabled the casualties to be evacuated by helicopter as soon as he had got them back.

On Christmas Day Johnnie accompanied an Iranian patrol moving forward from another defended area with the intention of seizing high ground near one of the main enemy positions.

They had gone 1000 yards when the leading troops of the patrol were attacked by an Adoo group in thick trees. The Arab officer of the Firquat Tariq Bin Zaid was killed in the opening burst of fire. A Firquat soldier picked up the dead body and attempted to carry him to the rear. Seeing that the man was having great difficulty, Johnnie handed his weapon to another soldier and picked up the body himself. Shortly afterwards he was heard to cry out as he fell to the ground mortally wounded. The intensity of the enemy's fire was so great that it was not possible to recover Johnnie's or the Arab officer's bodies for some time afterwards.

It was perhaps typical of the man that he should give his life attempting to recover the body of one of his comrades whilst under deadly aimed fire from a determined and ruthless enemy. I feel that his action typifies the magnificent courage and complete disregard of his own safety that Johnnie always showed.* Like so many who died in this little-known war, his gallantry and devotion to duty were beyond praise, and it was the deeds of such men that eventually brought victory to the Sultan and peace to this desert land.

In June 1974, as the swirling clouds rolled in from the Indian Ocean to cloak the *jebel*, I left Oman to face a different challenge: the Zaire River.

* Major J. B. Braddell-Smith was awarded the Sultan's Gallantry Medal, posthumously.

5. 'Dr Livingstone, I presume?'

'Dr Livingstone, I presume?' These immortal words, uttered by Henry Morton Stanley in 1871, had heralded a great chapter in the annals of exploration, and in 1943 they sent a shiver of excitement down my spine as I sat in Sunday school, attentive for once, listening to the gripping story.

David Livingstone, that remarkable Scot, had been found by an already successful journalist who was to become equally famous as a dogged, determined and ruthless explorer. Their meeting was indeed an historic occasion, which made a deep impression on Stanley, and during the four months he spent with Livingstone he learned much of the old missionary's discoveries, hopes and theories.

When, after his return to Britain, he heard of the doctor's death, Stanley said, 'May I be selected to succeed him in opening up Africa to a shining light of Christianity,' but his chief ambition was to pursue that last unfinished quest on which Livingstone had died – the search for the source of the Nile. We now know that John Hanning Speke had in fact found the principal source at the Ripon Falls on the northern shore of Lake Victoria in 1862; however, twelve years later the authenticity of Speke's discovery was still disputed by many of his contemporaries. Livingstone was among them; he believed that the Lualaba River, which he had found to the west of Lake Tanganyika, might itself be the Nile. The only way to test his theory was to follow the Lualaba's course, and Stanley resolved to do just that. Backed by the *Daily Telegraph* of London and his old paper, the *New York Herald*, he set out from Zanzibar in November 1874 with three other white men and 356 Africans. They carried an impressive quantity of weapons and the sectionalized wooden boat which Stanley named *Lady Alice* after his fiancée, a Miss Alice Pike of New York.

He kept a daily diary of his travels, and in the entry for 17 November 1874, defines his enterprise as the 'Anglo-American Expedition for the Discovery of the Nile and Congo Sources'. He was to cross the 'Dark Continent' from east to west. Throughout 1875 the expedition pressed on across Africa, circumnavigating and surveying the great lakes, driving off attacks by hostile tribes and marching, marching, marching. Little was known about the interior of Africa at this time, and in matters of detail the available maps could be compared with those of the moon's surface today. In October 1876, however, Stanley and his now severely depleted party reached the banks of the Lualaba at Nyangwe. Already he had taken heavy casualties; his men were exhausted and it is said that he spun a coin saying, 'Heads, I go forward, tails I go back.' Apparently it came up tails on two occasions but Stanley still decided to go on.

The explorer had reached the Lualaba some 550 miles from its source, in the swamps of what is now southern Zaire. The Lualaba is not, of course, any part of the Nile but the head-stream of the Congo. Together they form the mighty confluence which flows across central Africa to the Atlantic and is today known as the Zaire River.

Stanley had finally reached the Atlantic coast in August 1877. Two years later he returned to central Africa to play an important role in establishing what was recognized in 1885 as the Congo Free State. This was formerly annexed by Belgium in 1908 as the Belgian Congo, and in 1960 achieved independence as the Democratic Republic of the Congo. Finally, in 1971, after many internal vicissitudes, both the republic and its great river were given their present name of Zaire. It is in fact an old name, known to Europeans since the fifteenth century and derived from a Kikongo word which just means 'river'. 'Congo' is first encountered in the seventeenth century, being taken from the kingdom of Kongo which adjoined the river's lower course.

No detailed scientific work was carried out on Stanley's expedition and, in the years that followed, the vast Congo basin (as it is still internationally known) remained largely cloaked in dense tropical jungle and relatively inaccessible. Then in 1970 it was suggested that the Scientific Exploration Society (SES), the international cadre of explorers and scientists which we had established following our success on the

Blue Nile in 1968, should attempt to carry out a programme of medical and scientific research in this vast land, in commemoration of Stanley's epic journey.

It was obvious that with few roads in the area the best way would be to move by river, traversing most of the 2770 miles of the dangerous, rapid-strewn waters, much of which had not previously been navigated. So it was that whilst my attention was largely centred on the problems of the Darien Gap, I was also asked to lead the proposed expedition to Zaire at a future date. The late Prince William of Gloucester launched the venture at a dinner in the Grocers' Hall on 3 November 1971, the one-hundredth anniversary of Stanley's famous meeting with Livingstone. It was a splendid party and superbly organized, thanks largely to the help of our friends in the publicity department of the *Daily Telegraph*. There then followed three years of hard, problem-studded planning.

As soon as we had digested the reconnaissance report prepared by Martin Romilly and Richard Snailham, we invited Major-General Griff Caldwell to chair the expedition committee and also battle with the unenviable task of raising the money. Unlike a military operation, the expedition had to pay for everything in advance. It was rather like going into battle, but first of all having to raise the money to buy the ammunition. But with the experience of helping the Darien expedition behind him, General Griff soon recruited a powerful team for his committee. We were joined by Colonel Bruce Maude, formerly my commanding officer and now a well-known stockbroker, as treasurer. David Russell, chairman of a large advertising company, was to be a valuable ally, and we were most fortunate to have Morris Green, then editor of the *Daily Telegraph* and also formerly a Royal Engineer, with us. There were representatives too from the Foreign and Commonwealth Office, Survival–Anglia Television and the British Museum (Natural History).

Whilst I had been in Oman our London office had been run by a dear friend, Kay Thompson, and her daughter Jill. Also on our headquarters staff was an expert, dynamic fund-raiser, Donald Miles-Marsh, and a most charming and very professional publicity consultant named Roger Pemberton. Without the help of Denis Lowry, Bill Sansom, Brenda Rogers and Ken Monk, all at Gestetner's, I do not know how we should have coped. But there were literally masses of people who came to our aid and unselfishly gave valuable time and effort to help the project.

My first major task was to select the team and its equipment. Initially, I envisaged a small group, approximately forty-strong, to support the large number of scientists who would be so essential to our main purpose. However, our early studies of the area showed that the sheer scale of the country and its river would require a much bigger expedition. The Zaire is the seventh longest river in the world and the second biggest in its outflow, which averages 42 000 cubic metres per second! The country is the third largest in Africa, approximately the size of Western Europe, and it has one of the highest rainfall areas in the world. So the team expanded, eventually reaching a total strength of 165, including fifty scientists and nine women. We drew our members from all over the world, selecting them mainly for their compatibility and industry. People with experience of Africa and those with the knowledge of French or the local languages were especially sought after. Our final complement included Americans, Australians, Belgians, Britons, Canadians, Fijians, Frenchmen, Nepalese, New Zealanders and Danes. We also asked for a strong contingent of Zaïrois servicemen and scientists.

So many British scientists wanted to come with us that we had to run a long series of searching interviews, which were conducted with great patience and understanding by Dr Humphry Greenwood of the British Museum (Natural History), who had long done much to assist the Scientific Exploration Society. My main problem was that the scientists all wanted to go in different directions; also, because this was a genuine piece of exploration, I couldn't really give them the detailed information on the country which they really needed to plan their work.

The lady members of the team were particularly interesting. I certainly did not pick them to do the cooking and sewing. Three were scientists. A charming Australian bacteriologist, Beth Haslewood, was married to Professor Geoffrey Haslewood, another expedition member. We also had a French immunologist, Dr Madeleine Mojon, and from Leicestershire came Dorothy Bovey, one of the leading painters of botanical specimens, who was to provide illustrations for Kew Gardens.

There were three nurses. Marie-Thérèse Guichard, or Fifi as

we knew her, was a SAAFA sister with the British Army of the Rhine and was a qualified State Registered Nurse; although I only discovered half-way through the expedition that this was for mental nursing, nevertheless perhaps that was appropriate. A well-built Canadian girl, Adrianne Damgaard, was also an SRN and something of a physiotherapist. Certainly she was to work wonders on many a strained muscle in the months ahead, although one soldier complained that he went to Adrianne with a painful shoulder muscle and came back with a broken neck! A happy-go-lucky blonde nurse called Pamela Baker spoke fluent French as well as some Lingala and Swahili. She was the daughter of George Baker, one of our earliest supporters, who as Head of Chancery at the British Embassy at Kinshasa had done much to help our reconnaissance team. Pam had the ability to work twenty-three hours a day without food and possessed a tremendous sense of humour and sympathy. I reckoned anyone who had known President Mobutu and the people of Zaire was going to be especially useful, so I made her my personal assistant.

To record the vast amount of data that the scientists expected to collect we appointed two secretaries. Valerie Jones was a professional jockey from Scotland whilst Maggie Bush was the daughter of my old friend Brigadier Peter Bush, who at that time had just taken over as deputy commandant at Sandhurst. A seasoned explorer, Carolyn Oxton, who had helped us with the horses in Darien, could well have been especially useful if we had any animal transport, but in the end she spent her time working with the medical research team.

The most difficult job of all was to raise the £125 000 in cash that we needed to launch the project. I could write a book on that subject alone, but in the end we left for Zaire £20 000 short of our target; thanks to some stringent economy and some excellent fund-raising both in Britain and Zaire during the expedition, we only had to find £13 000 when we returned four months later.

Among the key members of our force was ex-Royal Marine Captain Mike Gambier, whom I had known for many years and appointed as my deputy. Major Derek Jackson, a thirty-five-year-old rugged and ruthless administrator, became commander of the important logistic support group, with Gordon Mitchell, a tough Scots Guards major, as quartermaster. Naturally there were many ex-Darien hands, including Major

Ernie Durey, the inexhaustible engineer who was to crack the land obstacles, and Captain Jim Masters, another sapper who was in charge of the fleet. Captain Peter Marett had been my intelligence officer on the previous expedition and I had no hesitation in asking him to join me in that role again. Advanced liaison in Zaire was assigned to a chum from Cyprus days, Major Tom Hawkins R E and his able assistant W O I Jim Winter. They had both been on a British Army training team in Zaire for several years and therefore knew the people and spoke French. The task of co-ordinating the administration of the scientific team was given to Major Ashley Barker, Royal Signals, whom I had known at Sandhurst. His team included a galaxy of experts with Freddie Rodger, a leading authority on tropical eye disease, directing the medical research group in looking for a cure for 'river blindness'.

Air support was a vital factor. Here another of our supporters, Lieutenant-General Sir Napier Crookenden, managed to obtain for us the assistance of the Army Air Corps, who kindly provided a Beaver light aircraft which was eventually to fly out to Africa on its own, crossing the Sahara on the way.

Gordon Mitchell, our utterly unflappable quartermaster, worked for long hours from his London office amassing over eighty tons of stores and supplies and, together with his aide, Lieutenant Dick Festorazzi, saw to its shipment to Africa. Whilst this was going on, the headquarters of the expedition had been established in a Whitehall cellar; in the end there were twenty-eight servicemen and civilians working in the small airless rooms fifty feet beneath the pavements.

1974 was not a good year to launch one of the most ambitious expeditions ever to leave Britain. Money was, to say the least, a trifle hard to find. The RAF were desperately short of aircraft and civil air charter rates were soaring. The price of petrol was rising daily, as indeed was the cost of almost everything. British Army units were hard-pressed and could ill afford to spare good men to go off on what some regarded as a jolly good swan. In Africa, political feelings were running high. The wind of change was sweeping through Angola and Mozambique. President Mobutu had recently nationalized the petrol companies in Zaire and former white settlers were leaving the country. Thus the pessimism of Europeans in Zaire about our project was understandable. Nevertheless, we believed it could be done and we went on planning. We decided, however, to change our name from the 'H. M. Stanley Centenary Expedition' to simply the 'Zaire River Expedition', quickly abbreviated by the military to ZRE.

The old SES formula appeared to be working once again: a thorough-going scientific expedition with the added spice of an attempt to run a dangerous river. A varied scientific programme made it all objectively worth while, and the prospect of heroics on the water attracted the media and the commercial sponsors whose support made it all possible.

Our use of the Zaire River was no gimmick. To move from Shaba (formerly Katanga) to the Atlantic with a vast team, scientific equipment, stores and a variety of nationalities was quite a problem. There are few roads or any means of communications in Zaire and therefore the river was the natural way. Indeed the Belgians had seen this in colonial times and had inaugurated a steamer service throughout the navigable parts. Where cataracts intervened – below Kinshasa, at the Stanley Falls and at the 'Gates of Hell' – they put down narrow-gauge railways around the obstacles. But if we were to move along the river then we had to find a way of getting through these cataracts, where the waves reached almost forty feet in places.

We had considered hovercraft but found these too low in carrying capacity and too costly in fuel. Derek Jackson had done a study of the possibility of using airships but they needed masses of helium which seemed to be in short supply in Africa. After much research and time spent on the Colorado River with an expert boatman named Ron Smith, Jim Masters had designed and assembled three giant thirty-seven-foot-long inflatable rafts from various bits obtained for us by Ron. They only had an air pressure of approximately two and a half pounds per square inch, and one of the problems that worried us most was how to apply enough power to these flabby craft. In the end we settled for two forty-horsepower Mercury outboard engines, mounted at either end of the boat.

However, our research did not stop there, and we were also provided with certain types of Avon inflatable boats and two rather unusual Hamilton water jetcraft which we used on the advice of Prince Philip. I believed that with a combination of these various craft we could tackle almost any rapid that we came against, and if, in the end, we could not get through, then

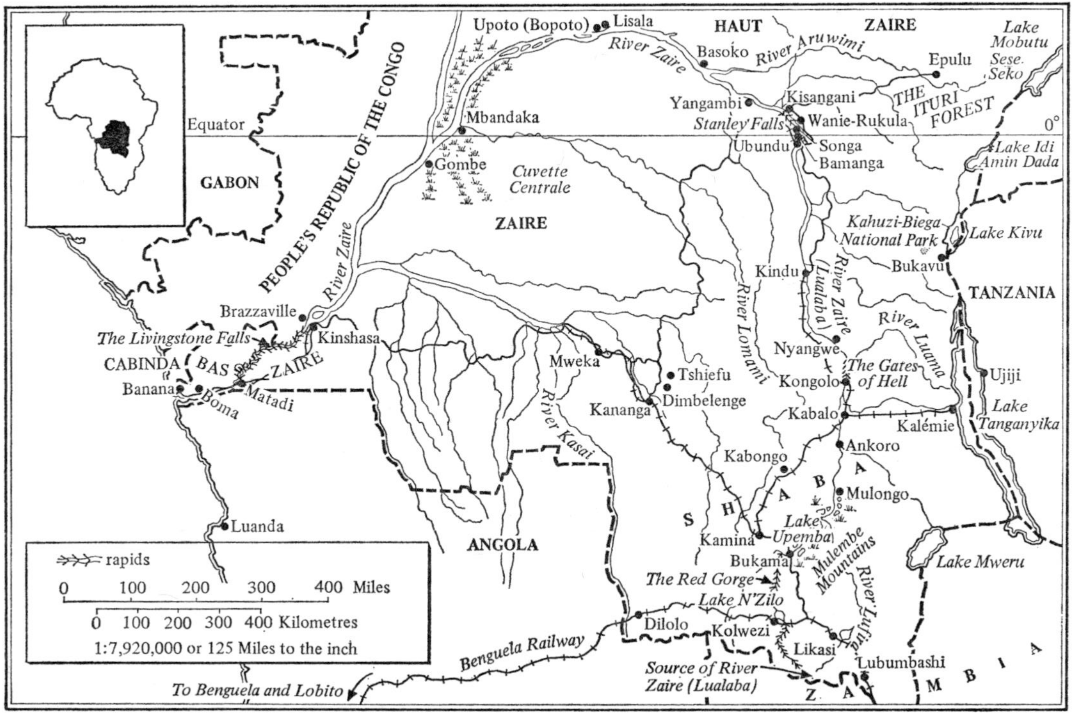
HAUT ZAIRE
Upoto (Bopoto)
Lisala
River Zaire
Basoko
River Aruwimi
Epulu
Lake Mobutu Sese Seko
THE ITURI FOREST
Kisangani
Yangambi
Stanley Falls
Wanie-Rukula
0°
Equator
Mbandaka
Gombe
Cuvette Centrale
Ubundu
Songa
Bamanga
Lake Idi Amin Dada
GABON
PEOPLE'S REPUBLIC OF THE CONGO
ZAIRE
Kahuzi-Biega National Park
Lake Kivu
Bukavu
Kindu
River Zaire (Lualaba)
TANZANIA
River Zaire
Brazzaville
Kinshasa
The Livingstone Falls
CABINDA
BAS ZAIRE
Banana
Boma
Matadi
Mweka
Tshiefu
Dimbelenge
Kananga
River Lomami
Nyangwe
River Luama
The Gates of Hell
Kongolo
Ujiji
Lake Tanganyika
Kabalo
Kalémie
River Kasai
Kabongo
Ankoro
Mulongo
SHABA
Lake Upemba
Kamina
Bukama
Mulembe Mountains
Luanda
ANGOLA
Lake Mweru
The Red Gorge
Lake N'Zilo
River Lufira
Dilolo
Kolwezi
Likasi
Lubumbashi
ZAMBIA
Benguela Railway
Source of River Zaire (Lualaba)
To Benguela and Lobito
rapids
0 100 200 300 400 Miles
0 100 200 300 400 Kilometres
1:7,920,000 or 125 Miles to the inch

Zaire

with the help of our Royal Engineers we should be able to portage round the difficult areas. By starting the expedition in October we hoped high water levels would cover the rocks. Two of our giant inflatables were sponsored by companies, and were therefore named *David Gestetner* and *Barclays Bank*.

Many of the lessons we had learned when navigating the Blue Nile in 1968 were remembered, and it was of great advantage having some of the old team with us again. No effort was spared to ensure our craft were the best available, though for experimenting we could find no suitable river to compare with the Zaire, and no rapids to match its cataracts. So in the end we could only hope and pray that our choice was right. Our lives depended on it!

The story of how we got the stores to Africa, through customs, overland and finally to where they were needed, is an epic in itself. However, much of the credit for it was due to the logistic support organization. Once there, we faced a river almost as long as the distance from Ireland to New York, and by the end of our voyage the scientists, medical research groups and boat parties would be split up as if they had one team in London, another in Athens and a third in Sicily. The lack of roads, railways, bridges and ferries did not help matters either, but our support group were to work tirelessly to win the logistics battle.

Communications were to be equally tenuous. We hoped the various teams and the fleet would be able to communicate with the support group on the relatively old A14 radios, but these are designed to operate over distances of up to 350 miles and were hardly suitable for the distances anticipated. However, they were all that was available and, apart from these, our signals section had only the civilian Racal sets with which to link us all together. Nevertheless, great credit is due to the Royal Signals detachment who, without complaint, managed to get our reports through to both the *Daily Telegraph* and the Ministry of Defence in London. We had also established a rear base in the capital, Kinshasa, to liaise with the Zaire army and government and to run a special expedition post office which had been set up by the Royal Engineers.

Linking up this scattered force were three eight-man, mobile, forward support teams (FST), each commanded by an experienced officer. It was their task to do advanced reconnaissance, establish good relations with the local people (who, after their experience of white mercenaries, were naturally rather suspicious) and to move stores, scientists and scientific specimens to and from the river. Each FST was to be responsible for one sector of the waterway. The whole operation was planned around the requirements of the various scientific parties, but because our experts could not be certain exactly where they would want to work, this plan had to be extremely flexible.

One hundred years before, Stanley had had a similar system but, lacking vehicles, he had been forced to use 700 men marching parallel to the river to support him. Nor did Stanley have the Beaver aircraft which we possessed. Fitted with the latest Sony video equipment and commanded by Cliff Taylor, a warrant officer in the Army Corps who had been with us in Panama, this robust six-seater plane was used for reconnaissance, parachute delivery of stores and aerial photography. One of its servicing team was Sergeant Ben Cartwright who had also been with us in Central America; he inscribed on its door the proud motto, '*Pas de problème*'. Even so, the local aviators did not envy them. Flying a single-engined aircraft out from Britain, over the Sahara, and spending four months operating above dense jungle with a country-wide fuel shortage, no diversionary airstrips, poor weather and no rescue facilities is not exactly a picnic. 'They'd never find you if you crashed in that cabbage anyway, so why worry?' smiled the cheerful second pilot, Flight Lieutenant Steve George RAF.

In early September the advance parties began to deploy – Tom Hawkins and one group to Lubumbashi and Derek to Lobito – to extract our vehicles and stores from the hold of a cargo ship and ferry them up the Benguela Railway to Zaire.

The journey out for the main party was one of the most amazing I have ever experienced. The day before we were due to depart my telephone in Whitehall rang and a voice at the other end said in poor English, 'This is Air Zaire, in Brussels.'

'Bonjour,' I replied with relief, for we had not heard anything for a considerable time from the company that was to fly us out, and I was beginning to wonder whether they would turn up.

'Please may we have permission to land in your country?' went on the slightly squeaky voice.

General Griff, who was sitting near me, grinned and nodded, so I simply said, 'Yes, when are you coming?'

'In about five minutes,' came the reply.

I was so staggered by this that I forgot to ask them where they were coming to, and it was Gatwick that got the shock when an enormous DC10 thundered in over their runway and parked up completely unannounced!

Gordon had taken great pains to see that all our stores were packed, weighed and listed with meticulous care. Nevertheless we seemed to be considerably overweight. Thus it was with some relief that, when our convoy reached Gatwick, the Zaire loadmaster rolled back his lips and waving aside any formalities of actually checking the cargo said, 'Stuff it all in, there is plenty of room.' Next morning three or four hefty guardsmen were still trying desperately to close the cargo doors against the bulging contents. However, we were soon airborne and as we undid our safety straps a smiling Zaïrois hostess came to me and said, 'Mon Colonel, may I have your permission to serve the champagne?'

Like Stanley* I said, 'Who pays?'

'Oh, it is with the compliments of the company,' she assured me and so they served champagne from Gatwick to Lubumbashi.

We did stop in Kinshasa to refuel with champagne and also to pick up one of our advance party, Captain Paul Turner, and our Zaire liaison officers (ZLOs). Paul, an energetic Hussar officer, had been in the capital for three weeks tying up all our final arrangements and had managed to establish a remarkable rapport with Muhammad Ali, who was then in Zaire preparing for his fight with George Foreman. As we flew on into the growing darkness of the African night I questioned the senior liaison officer, a Zaire parachute captain, on what he knew about the Shaba region.

'It is a very bad place,' he warned. 'They eat people down there,' he said, tapping his pistol meaningfully. Few of our ZLOs had ever visited the far-flung province; indeed it was rather like expecting a Londoner to know all about Castile!

I spent most of the flight, when not drinking the excellent champagne, learning a speech from Pam. My French is pretty

* When briefed by his employer, James Gordon Bennett, editor of the *New York Herald*, to go and find Livingstone, Stanley had asked, 'Who pays?' Bennett replied, 'Draw one thousand pounds now; and when that is spent, draw another one thousand and when you have finished that, draw another one thousand, and so on; but find Livingstone.'

abominable and so I had to write it out phonetically. The rest of the team enjoyed their last taste of luxury to the full!

It was long after dark when we touched down at Lubumbashi, and when the aircraft had stopped the doors were opened to let in the hot blast of African night air. Striding out on to the top of the steps I prepared to deliver my oration. There was only one problem – the airfield was deserted! However, an attractive Zaïrois lady stood at the foot of the steps and so I bounced down to her, extending my hand and, smiling, said, '*Enchanté, citoyenne.*'

As she returned my smile I heard Derek's voice coming from the darkness. He was running towards me and hissed, 'Not her, that's the airport whore.'

'What on earth have you done with customs and immigration?' I asked.

'Well, it is a long story, but they have all gone to a Burns Night supper,' he replied.

'Burns,' I gasped. 'But I shouldn't think they have ever heard of the immortal bard in Lubumbashi.'

'No, no,' he admitted, 'but we are paying for the supper, so they have all gone.'

Tom Hawkins and his advance party had managed to scrounge a motley collection of old vehicles from the town and in a very short time we had unloaded the aircraft, piled everything on to the trucks and set off towards our first base at the mining town of Kolwezi.

Thanks to the kindness of various expatriates and the authorities, we were made welcome; not only that, we were given accommodation in, by expedition standards, superb houses. On the first night of our sojourn I was the guest at a dinner given by a local businessman. The dinner was quite superb, and as the assembled company made their way on to the verandah with their cigars and brandy, one of the male guests said quietly to me, 'Colonel, I have been in Africa a very long time and I know why you are here. I would not presume to question your orders for one moment but I do hope that when the time comes you will call on me for assistance.'

'But we are here for a long-range scientific expedition,' I explained.

'My dear Colonel, with the utmost respect, when you have been in Africa as long as I, and when you have studied world affairs with the same interest as I, a businessman, have been forced to, you will learn to respect certain people. It is my opinion that for a very long time the British have been underestimated, and I congratulate your government on their present plans.'

Nothing I could say would convince the good fellow that we were not the forerunners of a massive British army that was to seize the mineral-rich province of Shaba. I tried, but he simply replied, 'I have looked carefully at your organization; you have a colonel, there are a great many majors, and you have radios, vehicles and a light aircraft. There is no doubt that you have the outline organization sufficient to raise an army in Africa tonight.' After two brandies I gave up and we joined the assembled company on the verandah.

Two days later Tom Hawkins came to me with a transport problem of considerable magnitude and therefore I instructed him to call upon this gentleman and request the use of his two large trucks.

'But those are the only vehicles he's got,' interjected Tom.

'I know,' I said, 'but just tell him I have need of them.'

Tom did as I bade and came back to me with surprise on his face, admitting that our friend had provided the vehicles without question!

On Sunday 6 October, using a local aircraft and taking Michael Gambier and Jim Masters with me, I flew south towards the Zambian border. Here I was able to examine the river and select a site from which we could launch the boats and start the expedition. As we wheeled over the narrow stream, Peter Marett took Polaroid pictures of the first rapids as well as the approaches to the launching site. There was a slightly tricky fall within a few miles of our starting point which worried me, but not as much as the bumpiness of our ride which made us all violently ill. Jim managed to hold out to the last, but unfortunately the sick-bag was full up by then and when he could wait no longer it was explained that there was no room left in the paper envelope!

At the base morale was high and everyone eager to be off, but there was still a great deal of preparation to be done. Whilst Derek and his team slaved away bringing forward the stores to our depot, the command element of the expedition continued with its reconnaissance.

On Monday 7 October we flew forward to Kongolo. I

wanted to view the rapids immediately north of Kolwezi. The initial expedition recce carried out by Richard and Martin in 1971 had warned me that these were very likely to be impassable, and I saw two bad falls in an enormous gorge of reddish rock that would certainly require portage. Peter Marett named it the 'Red Gorge' and marked it on the map. There were many rapids and, of course, the dams themselves that had been built to provide hydro-electricity for the copper-rich province. Portage would undoubtedly be necessary in a number of places until we came to the great mosquito-ridden swamps of Upemba. Here the problem would be navigation because it was difficult to see the course of the river!

Skimming over ground we spotted hippo, elephant and buck along the riverbank and then, at Kongolo itself, the foaming Gates of Hell. The water was dangerously low, and until the jagged black rocks were covered I was doubtful if we could sail through. However, when we landed at the local airstrip the people assured me that the water would rise within the month, although I wondered. There was no aircraft fuel available at Kongolo and therefore we were forced to fly on towards Lake Tanganyika, and eventually landed shortly before dusk at Kalemie (formerly Albertville). Lake Tanganyika, like a vast inland sea, azure blue with long, palm-fringed golden beaches, glimmered beneath us. After a night in the local hotel we awoke at dawn to find the streets outside lined with armed soldiers. As a flaming orange sun rose over the lake the troops moved off in vehicles on an operation, but the atmosphere was still tense and, although we were unarmed, people regarded us with suspicion. It was extremely fortunate that we had a ZLO with us and another useful asset was our special expedition arm badge which contained the symbol of the Mouvement Populaire de la Révolution and therefore indicated that at least we were on the side of President Mobutu.

Flying back to Kolwezi across the rising hills and savannah parkland we saw magnificent waterfalls and rapid-strewn rivers, all tributaries of the mighty Zaire. There were small herds of game dotted about the plain and, re-examining the area of the Red Gorge, I decided to deploy a bank reconnaissance group. The main lesson that I had learnt from this flight was that vast distances were involved in this enormous country; the logistic problems of this expedition had been highlighted. This was no Blue Nile or Darien Gap, with a few hundred miles of difficult terrain to be overcome, but a seemingly endless land of mountain, swamp, river and jungle sweltering in the equatorial heat. I concluded that wherever possible we must move by water and, therefore, it would be necessary to increase the size of the fleet that I proposed to assemble to the north of Bukama. The river was indeed the key to movement, but Derek would have to achieve miracles to support us.

As we neared our base I must have fallen asleep for suddenly I awoke with a searing pain on the right side of my head and, before I knew what had happened, my eardrum had burst, undoubtedly due to the rapid descent with a mild head cold. The discomfort which followed was a wretched nuisance, especially as we had such a busy time and as I was to speak that evening at a dinner given by the Lions Club of Kolwezi. Everywhere we went people, both black and white, were friendly and hospitable. In fact, there was a considerable demand for us to show films of our previous expeditions which, luckily, we had with us. Tom Hawkins's deep Scots voice was often heard haranguing the inhabitants in French on the terrors of the Panama jungle. Indeed, by passing the hat round on these occasions we were even able to raise some money for our depleted funds!

The first part of the expedition was to navigate the upper reaches of the river. Here, with our base still at Kolwezi, we proceeded downstream in the Avon Professional inflatables. These excellent boats were steered by long sweep oars and the occasional use of small Johnson outboard motors. The team had some ferocious water to navigate and experienced a great many thrills and spills. When it came to the waters of the Red Gorge many of the younger men wanted to try to get through in the boats. It was the old 'hawks and doves' situation which we had experienced on the Blue Nile, and I had to make a firm ruling that we were not here to commit suicide but to get on with an expedition. The hawks grumbled but the doves realized the wisdom of this decision.

Meanwhile our whole team was being controlled by Tac HQ (tactical headquarters). This consisted of Peter Marett, as intelligence officer, and Pam Baker, my long-suffering PA, together with Sam Qarau, the Fijian corporal of the Queen's Own Hussars, who was our signaller. When Sam was introduced to Pam he said, without blinking, 'I believe we must be related.'

'How do you make that out?' asked the surprised blonde.

'Well, you see, my grandfather once ate a missionary called Baker,' remarked Sam.*

There were, of course, minor problems with our Zaire friends. Understandably enough they didn't really comprehend us at this stage, and one or two of the more politically inclined were highly suspicious. There was one officer, in particular, who perhaps unwittingly was wont to stir up trouble. I therefore had no choice but to gently ease him into a new position. Accordingly I instructed Peter Marett, a prodigious walker, to take him on a forty-mile hike to examine the Red Gorge. Peter set off with our friend and returned two days later, carrying him. We never saw this gentleman again and the political problem ceased to exist.

The river party, with its scientists, went on, crashing and tumbling through the foaming white water in the Katanga gorges. Whilst they were doing this I was deploying the rest of the expedition on land to support them and prepare the giant rafts for launching at Bukama. Mike Gambier, my able second-in-command, was in charge, and amongst the many exciting incidents that they had was one with a hippopotamus. The Royal Marines had decided to inspect the creature, which was situated with her calf in mid-river. The hippo did not take kindly to this and charged. With her first bite she destroyed the bow, with her second she got the stern and with her last, she destroyed what was left amidships; after this you don't have a boat and the Royal Marines baled out into another craft. They almost left behind Basil Pratt, our Army padre, who was at that moment in communication with his head office! When they looked back they saw a very perplexed hippo which, having just eaten an inflatable boat, was now suffering from a disastrous attack of wind.

Although many of our number had been with me on previous expeditions and were extremely experienced, as always we brought in fresh blood, particularly junior officers and young soldiers, so that they too might learn the ropes. It was very comforting to see how well the team moulded together in these early and rather trying days.

* A missionary, the Rev. George Baker, had indeed been eaten in Fiji, but was not related to Pam.

At the small riverside town of Bukama the river was wide enough for us to launch the giant inflatables. Resembling outsized rubber mattresses, these silver-painted boats' dimensions depended on how hard you blew them up. The minimum crew was only three, but each raft could carry up to thirty people. In addition there was fuel, rations, scientific equipment, radio sets, line-carrying rockets, engineer stores and tools, plus television cameras, artist's materials and medical stores to be stowed securely aboard.

On the flagship, *La Vision*, we also carried a yellow fibreglass six-wheeled, two-seater ATTEX amphibian. In charge of this 'buggy' was Paul Turner, who had obtained it by unknown means in Kinshasa. It was a useful vehicle which allowed us to get about more easily in the swamps and along some of the flood-plains.

The smaller craft in our fleet consisted of the close reconnaissance section's two Avon S400 boats. These were twelve-foot, fast, inflatable dinghies powered by forty-horsepower Johnson outboards. The section's task was to scout ahead of the big rafts and, when required, to find a safe way through the rapids. Commanded by Alun Davies, a cheerful captain in the Royal Regiment of Wales, they were a hard-working bunch who undoubtedly enjoyed the flexibility and speed of their little boats compared with the lumbering rafts which they led. In addition there was the engineer section commanded by Ernie Durey. This bunch of sappers were the greatest selection of piratical rogues on the river. They moved with their own boats and vehicles almost at will throughout the country. Their task was to ferry Land-Rovers across the rivers, build bridges, dynamite obstacles, transport scientists, collect fresh water and locate stocks of beer. All this they did admirably and with great success.

From Bukama I hoped to be able to reach Kinshasa, 2000 miles away, without taking our giant rafts off the river. But sailing into the flat, treeless waste of the Upemba swamp I was extremely worried that the water in the Gates of Hell might still be too low for navigation. Stanley's boat, the *Lady Alice*, had been built in sections for ease of overland movement. Our giant inflatables were collapsible, but the central float chamber, shaped like an elongated doughnut, weighed 750 pounds even when deflated. I discussed the problems of portaging with Jim Masters, a man whose judgement I respected enormously. We agreed that portaging would be a devil of a problem and that we must try to stay on the water as long as possible. We were also somewhat concerned about passing through the rocky Gates themselves. However, our padre assured us that with our sins they would be wide open!

6. Through the Gates of Hell

As we cruised through the still water of the great Upemba swamp, birds wheeled around us and the occasional crocodile slithered from the muddy islets. However, our main worry was still the ubiquitous hippo.

Early one evening a fearful tropical storm broke just as we were making camp. Thunder roared and lightning flashed as the rain drove into every shelter. Initially I managed to get some cover underneath a groundsheet but was soon drenched to the skin. Then I heard the sound of music and the clink of a bottle from *Barclays Bank*, moored near by. Without further thought, I bounded across from my flagship and landed on a small group of people huddled beneath a canvas. Pam, Maggie, Roger Chapman, Doug Newby and Dick Festorazzi were seeing the storm out with the aid of Neil Diamond and a bottle of Portuguese *vino verde*. We all squeezed beneath the shelter, which was barely sufficient to cover one person, whilst the tempest raged. Eventually, in spite of the discomfort we fell into a deep slumber. It must have been about four o'clock in the morning when an ear-splitting snort close at hand awoke us. Peering out into the night I perceived, only ten feet away, the glistening body of a bull hippopotamus. He was enraged because we were blocking his only exit from the river. Already our ZLOs were rushing from their bashas and cocking automatic weapons, but Dick Festorazzi thrust the electric loudhailer into my hand and said, 'Try that, it might have the same effect on him as it does on us.' 'Pee-eep-pee-eep' screamed the device as I flicked the siren switch to full volume. With a startled roar, the hippo fled up river.

At dawn the sodden, weary fleet continued its voyage. Engineers attended to maintenance, scientists to their research, Alun Davis to his reconnaissance and Pam to her many duties as my PA, one of which was writing up the daily log.

The entry for Tuesday and Wednesday, 29–30 October 1974 reads as follows:

Early morning palm-wine ceremony when chief arrived with bottles from village. Custom demanded I take a sip of this extremely alcoholic beverage. Did so with no ill effects although others who indulged suffered badly later! Decided we should sail through the night to save time as scientists not especially interested in the stretch immediately ahead. To save petrol, took aboard logs with which to make fires for cooking.
Navigation: distance run during daylight, 55 km; distance run during night, 38 km; total 93 km. Fleet arrived at Kalombo 2235 hours on 29 October. Location 8° 18.1′ S, 26° 19.2′ E. Terrain: typical swamps, river beginning to break up into many islands.
Entomology: rich in insects!
Anthropology: found sites rich in pottery from fifth to ninth centuries; reports of at least two skeleton sites.
Medical: general health on expedition continues good. Eye surgeon Dr John Chapman-Smith saw approximately thirty patients in Kalombo. Some children quite sick with wide variety of illnesses.
Zoology: heavy storm in Upemba Lake has caused death of many fish. Probably due to deoxidization of water when stirred up. Mormyrids and cichlid population in Lake Kisale collected. Olive baboon and hippo seen. Many purple herons and open-billed storks. Fish eagle and black-shouldered kites seen. Acides flies' eggs found.
Vegetation: papyrus studied in three lakes, growth pattern and performance differs greatly in these three sites. There is unique pattern of metabolism of photosynthesis found in the eight types of grasses in the swamps.
Local Catholic mission school visited the fleet in afternoon and spent an hour looking at boats. We briefed them on expedition and told of Scientific Exploration Society's work in the world.
People very friendly and we had a soccer match with them. Their team the local champions, named the Serpents, won easily; good time had by all; in evening attended dancing arranged in town in our honour. Mail, very welcome, arrived by Beaver. Also urgently needed supply of biscuits.
Cash and fuel situation growing worse and causing me real concern. Sent small party to visit the chief of Kikondja during day and tried to get fuel. They had no success but returned with beer. Chief apparently most congenial. Continued sailing through the vast marsh and on through the night. Heavy rain is frequent after dark and the storms dramatic. Fantastic thunder and lightning. Hippo still numerous.

By sailing at night we certainly saved time but did create other problems for ourselves. Once, when proceeding after dark, I noticed one of our lady members making her way towards the stern. This had been set aside for privy purposes because we had no inflatable loo and to go into the bank for this function would only mean dumping those in need up to their chests in mud! Suddenly the night was split by an awful scream; I thought for a moment that the poor woman had fallen overboard. But when she returned to the bridge I discovered the real reason. A ZLO, unable to understand English, had, alas, chosen to sleep in the scuppers at the stern of the craft.

'What on earth happened?' I asked.

'Oh! How the hell do you expect me to see a Zaïrois on a dark night?' she retorted.

Each day our scientists would explain their work to us. This was most helpful because on such an adventurous project it is easy to forget that the results of lasting value are those achieved by the experts. Captain Scott had said of his last polar expedition that he believed it was primarily a great scientific project, with the Pole as the bait for public support. Similarly, I believed that, although the navigation of the river was most important, the newsworthy challenge was also necessary to gain us funds for the entire operation. Several of our scientists had been unable to obtain financial grants from the institutions who usually support such work and therefore we also needed to raise money for them.

Although immediate results are not easy to obtain from our research, some of the subjects under scrutiny were fascinating. One project concerned the famous mountain gorilla. These enormous creatures can reach up to thirty stone and are only found in the high-altitude forests of Zaire. Tac HQ had been seeking information on their whereabouts and, one night in a small bar, Pam met a local official who claimed to have expert knowledge of the animals. However, we had no map with us and it was difficult to find out exactly where he thought they resided. The quest was not made any easier by the fact that this gentleman had consumed a considerable amount of Simba beer; as he did not speak English, I left him being interrogated by Pam. On return a few moments later I found her with her back pressed hard against the bar. The Zaïrois was attempting to describe where we might find the gorillas. To do this he was using the map of Africa on her T-shirt. As she edged closer and closer to the bar she whispered to me, 'I'll need rescuing before he reaches the Cape of Good Hope!'

However, one of our experts, Jeremy Mallinson, right-hand man to Gerald Durrell at the Jersey Zoo, was eventually treated to a rare opportunity when he spent five days in close proximity to a large family of mountain gorillas in dense forest in the highlands. Whilst there, one enormous male, who had been named Casimer, suddenly gave a deep roar and, beating its chest, charged to within six feet of Jeremy before calling off the attack! These bluffing tactics are well known in gorillas and Jeremy stayed put long enough to get a very splendid photograph. Another expert on primates, stocky, rugged Scotsman Sinclair Dunnett, spent his time seeking the rare pygmy chimpanzee and, eventually, after months of pains-taking searching over many hundreds of miles, managed to capture three of the quaint little creatures. These are believed to be the first ones ever caught for zoological research. On many of his journeys he was assisted by one of the Army's survival experts, Sergeant Major Eddy McGee, who had been with me in Oman. The sergeant major was certainly in his element and spent his time building hair-raising home-made traps that were terror to all in the area, including us!

On the river our geologists, both Zaïrois and British, studied rocks. Zaire has a great wealth of minerals, and in some places we saw whole hills of what looked like solid copper. Mean-while, the fish team sought their specimens with nets and lines. Professor Geoffrey Haslewood, biochemist at Guy's Hospital Medical School, spent many hours each day trying to collect samples for his study of fish bile, but in desperation had to get the sappers to speed up the work with the aid of a little dynamite. Dr Roger Sweeting, a research fellow at St John Cass College, was concerned with parasites; he also managed to acquire two black kites, which he named Biggles and Cromwell. The soldiers readily took to helping the fish team, and a day's netting became a popular pastime.

There were a great many problems when we arrived at Kongolo. The giant inflatables were using between five and ten gallons of petrol per day and there was simply no more to be had anywhere in Zaire. Somehow Derek Jackson had found a train, filled it with fuel and, doubtless contravening a number of regulations, had got it to the river. So when I arrived I found a base already established with adequate petrol for us to tackle the Gates of Hell. Meanwhile the sappers were still battling to get the overland convoys through on the terrible roads from Kolwezi. To complicate matters, Cliff Taylor, in charge of our aircraft, had been badly burned when a petrol cooker exploded. He looked a terrible mess and I feared for his future. But, thanks to Dr Ian Young's skill, Cliff was back in his cockpit within a week.

On our way north we had passed through Mulongo, where we had met two charming missionaries – Mary Goodsell, who had come out from Britain forty-four years previously, and Dolly MacDonald from Australia who had been there for a mere twenty-eight! Together they ran the Protestant mission and were extremely hospitable to us. At the mission everything looked serene and peaceful and I enjoyed one of those blissful periods of relaxation that are, alas, a rare privilege for expedition leaders.

The price of local petrol had now rocketed to the equivalent of £2.50 per gallon, even if you could get it! And it was only by achieving miracles that FST commanders like John Benham-Crosswell were able to go ahead of us and keep the whole circus moving. One of the Avon M650 boats had gone missing during the journey from Britain and we'd had to replace this with a Professional. Nevertheless, the performance of the raft, which was the same one that we had used in Darien, was only slightly impaired as a result of the modification, and ferrying operations continued under the able guidance of Ernie and his men.

At Mulongo I became increasingly concerned about the threat of the terrorists in the forests near the rapids. The commanding officer of a local battalion told me that he had suffered many casualties and warned me to be prepared for trouble. He hinted darkly that it would suit the terrorists very well to ambush us as we went through the worst of the rapids. Captain Kayalo, our senior ZLO, had recently returned from the capital with a large consignment of arms which Gordon Mitchell had wisely decided to keep under his control in large boxes labelled SCIENTIFIC INSTRUMENTS! However, I now took the decision to issue the 'instruments' and chose the Catholic mission as the distribution point. It was perhaps unfortunate, because this mission had been the scene of the most horrible massacre on 1 January 1962 when twenty-two priests had been taken out, had their throats cut and, it was said, been eaten by rebels during an uprising. When the inhabitants saw us receiving weapons they suspected that retribution was about to take place and fled! However, as a result of our gunboat diplomacy, no one had to use a weapon in anger, nor were we fired on at any time. Nevertheless, a few months after we had left the area, Jane Goodall, the chimpanzee expert, had her camp attacked in Tanzania and a number of her students were kidnapped and held to ransom in Zaire. So the terrorists got their publicity after all, but thankfully not at my expense.

In spite of our misgivings the Gates of Hell did not turn out to be such a severe obstacle after all. However, one native was clearly convinced we were going to our deaths for, having failed to stop us with wild gesticulations, he simply stood looking down and made the sign of the cross as we passed through the foaming water between the reefs of black rocks. Our boats proved to be as excellent as we had hoped and we sailed on, enjoying a slightly bumpy, but otherwise uneventful, ride in what could have been very dangerous water.

On 10 November we emerged from the final cataract of this stretch. Marc Smith, our young river-runner from the Colorado, was disappointed that the water had not yet really tested his ability. He came to see me, wishing to go home, but after a long conversation I was able to persuade him that the dangers and hazards of the Livingstone Falls that lay ahead would test even the bravest of us.

As we passed downriver the banks were crowded with villagers in brightly coloured clothes cheering and waving excitedly. They had come from miles around to see the first boats ever to sail through the rapids and as it was midday we pulled in for our lunch. Chiefs came on board and were offered lemonade powder and Army biscuits, thinly spread with Shippam's paste! The greetings over, the chiefs announced that their people wished to sing to us, which they did. Squadron Leader Mike Barnard, our musical navigator, found it too good an opportunity to miss and unwrapped his saxophone to give a rendering of 'Sweet Sue', which sent the people clapping with applause.

That night we camped on a grassy bank looking across what was now a slow-moving river almost 1000 yards wide, to a low ridge in the east. It was from this point that Stanley had first viewed the river in 1876 when his expedition had almost crossed two-thirds of Africa. As we cooked powdered egg into omelettes at breakfast, the local chiefs arrived by canoe. These thirty-foot-long craft were each propelled by twenty paddlers who worked in unison, chanting as they dug in their blades. Boats like this had been used by hostile natives to attack Stanley, but to us the people showed nothing but kindness. Indeed the fresh rations that they brought were a welcome change from the dehydrated versions.

On the fleet the pets multiplied. Ken Mason, the expedition's leading humorist and an ace photographer from the *Daily Telegraph*, had bought a small grey furry bushbaby named Tiddlypush for Pam. Being a nocturnal animal it was kept inside her shirt during daylight hours and on one occasion, when she was interpreting for me with a rather truculent chieftain, I noticed to my amazement that the man's eyes had suddenly come out on organ stops! The reason was simple: Pam's bosom was heaving up and down in a most remarkable fashion and then suddenly Tiddlypush emerged from her neckline. The chief fled and we had no more trouble!

On 13 November we reached the village of Nyangwe, near where Stanley had launched the *Lady Alice* after his march from Zanzibar, and where Dr Livingstone had lived for almost a year, trying in vain to persuade the local people to take him downriver. Then, after witnessing a most dreadful slaughter by Arab slavers, the doctor had marched back to Ukiji on Lake Tanganyika where Stanley had found him, sick and weak, in 1871. In the field behind Nyangwe were graves of Belgian soldiers who had died fighting in the Force Publique, which Stanley had set up in the 1880s to defend the new Congo Free State. Ironically, these men had perished whilst driving out the slavers under the infamous Tippu-Tib, who had supported Stanley in 1876. As we stood in the long grass viewing the monument and its simple plaques, there was a movement on the brickwork. A thin green snake rose from the grass and slithered up to the top of the plinth, coiled itself and raised its head to hiss menacingly at us. We left the tombs with their sinister guardian and returned to the river.

Snakes were by no means uncommon and we had found several on the banks and on an occasion spotted one swimming across the river. I shouted to Bob Powell, commanding a nearby recce boat, 'Catch it!' He did, with the aid of a plastic bag and a paddle, and on getting it into the boat found that what he had landed was a spitting cobra. This deadly beast can throw its venom with accuracy for some eight feet and so three men ended up in the water and the snake stayed in the boat!

Thanks to the ever-watchful eye of our fleet's medical officer, Dr John Chapman-Smith, we were always alert for disease. We knew that we were riding one of the biggest sewers in Africa and all drinking water had to be filtered, boiled and sterilized. Indeed it was safer to drink whisky, of which fortunately we had an abundance. Nevertheless, fevers did occur and one of our early patients was Pam who, having nursed a Gurkha suffering from chicken pox, now caught the bug herself. For days she lay beneath an improvised canopy that Jim Masters erected on the flagship to shield her from the relentless African sun.

Meanwhile we pressed on towards Kindu, scene of more modern tragedies of the 1960s, for it was here that the drug-crazed Simba rebels had started their revolt, through which they eventually seized large areas of the country. The hard-working *Commissaire du Zone* greeted me with a bottle of Scotch and entertained us royally. He had already been chatted up by John Benham-Crosswell who had arrived earlier with his FST and, understandably, had been mistaken for a group of mercenaries. However, all was now well and the people of Kindu extended to us the most wonderful hospitality.

Of course, we always made efforts to ensure that there were good relations with the locals. Captain Kabe, a Zaire naval officer, would often say to me when we docked in any small town, 'John, I think I shall go ashore to look into Naval matters.' He normally returned at dawn, usually with two attractive girls on his arm, and when I would ask him, 'Naval matters all right, Captain?' he would reply with a great grin, 'Number one, number one.'

From time to time in our travels local officials would make the normal gesture of offering me, as commander of the expedition, the gift of a few local ladies. Over a period of time I had learnt most of the excuses in the book – 'My religion doesn't permit it', 'I am not feeling very well', 'My wife would not approve' – but in one particular town, when I had exhausted all possibilities, Pam suggested that I hand the matter over to one of our able Zaire sergeants. I explained to him the cause of my embarrassment and asked if he would help me out.

'*Mais certainement, mon Colonel*,' he replied. Next morning the sergeant in question arrived at Tac HQ, saluted and explained that he was ready to provide his services in the cause of the expedition whenever required. As a result we escaped many a tricky situation and had the most faithful senior NCO of the Zaire Army!

For much of our journey we had been passing through bush country, but on 14 November a solid wall of tall trees rose suddenly on both banks and we entered the jungle. At Kindu our entomologists, assisted by our Gurkhas, set up a camp in the tropical rain-forest. The entomologists were sampling the flying insects at different levels between the top of the trees and the ground. They believed that this study would give them the first overall indication of the composition, vertical distribution and richness of the flying insect fauna of the rain-forest canopy in central Africa. Such knowledge is essential in order to assess the importance of the forest as a natural resource. Working closely with a team of Zaire scientists, some of the best in the land, who had been sent on the orders of the president to join us, our experts set electrically powered ultra-violet light traps to collect the insects at different heights above the ground. In order to get the traps up into the trees a small team of sappers were employed as climbers. One of these, Sergeant Mick Hough, managed to survive an eighty-five-foot fall! It was not surprising that he was from the parachute engineer squadron and, after some ten minutes' unconsciousness, stood up, shook himself and mouthed one or two expletives. We later discovered that he had a minor brain haemorrhage and a split liver, but the fact that he survived was a miracle.

At ground level our scientists were to discover many interesting creatures, including fascinating butterflies, colourful moths and some highly dangerous snakes. Major Michael Gallagher found a deadly forty-two-inch gaboon viper, the bite of which gives you approximately three seconds to hand your best friend your wallet!

Supplying these groups in the forest was never easy and usually involved long difficult journeys by Land-Rover or parachute drops from the Beaver. Nevertheless they ate quite well, making up the deficiencies of their diet with monkeys provided by the ZLOs. It was never a taste which I enjoyed but, having sampled it before in the Darien Gap, I could put up with it. On another occasion I brought them a bottle of whisky. The scientists' eyes lit up with glee. It was unfortunate that the water they used to top up the liquor had been tainted with formalin: the lot were almost pickled for posterity!

Meanwhile, back at Kindu, Derek's logistic team were working hard to keep the whole show on the road. They had all sorts of frustrations, including one when a train started off in the wrong direction and no one could speak the same language as the engine driver. On another occasion a thief stole a video battery and was caught by a Zaire sergeant. Justice was done immediately and seen to be done, for the poor fellow was thrashed mercilessly in front of us before being taken off to the magistrate for sentence. As the battery had expired anyway I sent a note to the court to ask for clemency for the wretched man. The magistrate respected my wishes and only gave him a year's penal servitude.

Four hundred miles away, in a remote village, Freddie Rodger, as senior medical officer, was leading the medical research team investigating many diseases, including river blindness,* which afflicts more than two million people. His inquiry was unusual in that apart from the study of the natives for eye damage and the telltale skin nodules which accompany the infection that leads to river blindness, his team were also studying the environment of the endemic areas.

It was a pathetic sight to watch the queues of people outside the head man's straw hut awaiting examination; some blind, many already heavily disfigured by the subcutaneous lumps. The only light relief was the arrival of four Pygmies, who politely declined Freddie's invitation to have their eyes looked at on the grounds that he would be able to glimpse their souls!

The researchers' efforts were directed at finding clues towards a cure for the disease, which is caused by the bite of a black fly known as *Simulium damnosium*, so the background of each person was thoroughly investigated, even down to the number of wives. Freddie was there to find where onchocerciasis was most prevalent; although he had originally planned to be with us on the river, on arrival in Zaire he had discovered that the main centre for the affliction was some 400 miles away. It was fortunate, therefore, that our operation was so flexible and that we could cope with the sudden changes in plan that were necessitated by the scientific programme.

* The results of this work are in *Onchocerciasis in Zaire*, edited by F. C. Rodger (Pergamon, 1977).

At Kindu we refitted the boats from the quartermaster's train for the next obstacle. The stores were certainly unique. In a railway siding guarded by Zaire soldiers stood a 'wagon-lits' and a collection of closed trucks. The quartermaster paraded up and down with a large stick. Men approached at their peril, but when the custodian of all we possessed decided that an issue should be made, it was a great moment. A huge bunch of keys were produced and, like a medieval jailer, Gordon Mitchell would stride up to the selected wagon, which might bear the magic sign G1098.* The heavy steel doors would slide open, revealing a host of goodies. Few were permitted the privilege of actually entering the inner sanctum.

Meanwhile over the radio to Kinshasa I heard that the jet-boats had arrived early. The New Zealand team under Jon Hamilton were anxious to get on with the job of reconnoitring the Livingstone Falls as early as possible. Time spent in reconnaissance is never wasted, especially on expeditions, but I was not yet prepared to have an FST deployed that far ahead. Already our force was getting something like 1000 miles in length! However, the jets were there and so I made plans to send forward John Benham-Crosswell and his team. At the same time I had to replace Tom Mabe who had been skippering *Barclays Bank*. He was one of the few men with expert knowledge of what our giant rafts could accomplish on this tricky river and I needed him to look at the Stanley Falls ahead of us and also, of course, the Livingstone Falls that were going to be the real test in the months ahead. Thus I brought in Billy Bowles, a yachting cavalryman from Bill Coleridge's FST, to take over command of *Barclays Bank*.

While all this reorganization was going on Sinclair Dunnett and a tough marine named Bob Hudson were still pursuing the rare pygmy chimpanzee down the Lomami River that ran parallel and to the west of the Zaire. At night we would receive faint reports from them by radio, but in spite of the most terrible privations they had not yet found the elusive creatures. We supplied them by air and kept our fingers crossed that nothing serious would occur, for they were well outside the range of any immediate help.

In Kindu I met the charming president of the local Luncheon Club, who mentioned that she also ran the cinema, night club and brothel. She invited me to dinner the next day. I inquired

* Army terminology for general stores

if I might bring with me one or two friends (for safety) and so, accompanied by Pam and Captain Kabe, went to her house the following evening. She and her sister, their hair arranged in spikes, had prepared a delightful meal of traditional Zaire dishes. We were half-way through dinner when I felt something touch my leg. It was more than that; it was quite clearly a hand which, very gradually as the meal progressed, worked its way up the inside of my trousers. I was slightly alarmed and, looking across to the lady opposite, was intrigued by the fact that both her hands were on the table. Eventually when the fingers had almost reached my knee I could stand it no longer and easing my chair back shot my arm under the table to grasp whatever it was. Out came a very tiny chimpanzee dressed in a sailor suit and furious at having been disturbed.

'Ah, you have found poor Sophie,' said madam.

'She must be a very young chimpanzee,' I replied.

'Ah no, she is very old,' insisted the lady.

Thus it was that whilst Sinclair and Bob were undergoing a separate and most trying expedition, I had found a pygmy chimpanzee under a table in Kindu!

Whenever the expedition was forced to camp in or near a large town there were problems of accommodation. The Zaïrois authorities were naturally anxious to give us the best possible houses. However, to get the whole group into one building was impossible and we normally ended up being scattered over a wide area. Usually I had to accept the bungalow that they pressed on my Tac HQ. Often it was far better than those given to the rest of the expedition and I felt embarrassed about it, but the advantage was that it gave me better overall control and allowed me a certain amount of privacy to deal with the delicate problems that arose almost hourly. It did tend to make me a little out of touch with members of the fleet, who were normally accommodated elsewhere. The problem was that with such a large party we simply could not be based in one place when we were in a town; this was only possible in the jungle where things were much simpler.

Whilst the fleet moved from Kindu to Ubundu under Mike Gambier I had gone off to see Freddie and cope with the administrative problems that now plagued us. Finally I flew on to Ubundu in the Beaver and landed just before half light to be met by Joe Tuwai, another of our cheery Fijian NCOs. Motoring along a forest trail to the town, we came upon a group of large apes. For a moment I thought we were facing gorillas but they were almost certainly wild chimpanzee, and as I leapt out to follow them up, they disappeared, chattering, into the bush. But not before I had noticed that their coats of hair were much thicker than is usual with captive creatures.

Near Ubundu was a Christian mission headed by the lively Father Augustine. He was the only survivor from a Simba attack during the revolt. He was alive today simply because he had been away on leave and had returned to find that everyone else had been killed. We had a most interesting evening talking to him and learning about the area, including reports of crude oil seeping from the ground near by. However, I was ashamed to hear of all the alleged activities of a small canoe expedition who had passed through on the easier stretches of the river earlier. Apparently they had rather 'ripped off' some of the Europeans they had met at missions along the river.

Everywhere we went on this stage of the journey there were reminders of the civil war: burnt-out tanks, crashed aircraft, destroyed bridges and ferries and deserted hospitals and churches. It was a sad scene and it is good to know that today President Mobutu's government are trying hard to restore this area to its former levels of prosperity.

The Stanley Falls starting at Ubundu consisted of a stretch of some seven cataracts over a distance of fifty miles. The usual reconnaissance had been carried out by air, land and river, and, in spite of local stories that the river went underground, we did not expect too much trouble. How wrong we were.

Ken Mason was snapping members of the flagship's crew as we passed through some moderate rapids. Suddenly, without warning, all hell let loose.

'Look out,' yelled Peter Marett, who had seen that we were about to plunge into a yawning fourteen-foot-deep chasm which inexplicably had opened up in the riverbed.

Already one of the Avon dinghies was in the boiling pit being hurled about like a cork in a washtub. Now the giant raft on which I was riding came crashing down the slope and a huge wave swamped our engine, hurling the sapper helmsman, Sergeant Bob Russell, off his feet. A wall of water struck the bow, sweeping away precious stores, including a number of waterproof camera boxes that had been lashed in with 1000-pound-breaking-strain wire. The decking boards splintered beneath us as the great raft flexed and twisted in the cauldron.

'We're breaking up,' shouted someone.

With no engine we were trapped in the hole, being pounded by mountains of brown water that spun us around so that one lost all sense of direction. Then, for no apparent reason, we were thrown clear to drift into slack water. It was a great relief, but behind us the second Avon dinghy had already gone into the swirling funnel and I'd just time to see Richard Snailham's bearded face aghast with horror as he held on for dear life. *Barclays Bank*, the second big boat, skilfully steered by Billy Bowles, managed to avoid the hole, but the *David Gestetner* went straight in. We watched anxiously as momentarily she stood on her bow.

'She's going over,' I thought, but miraculously the giant fell back into the pit and escaped.

Next day, we went to the village of Songo and tried to send a message forward offering a reward for any of the various pieces of kit that we had lost that might be recovered. Although they had no telephones we found that the local talking drums were quick and efficient and for the equivalent of fifty pence you could get ten minutes on a talking drum in the cheap period! Even our signals officer was full of admiration for the work of the sweating drummers who claimed they could communicate up to thirty miles by night and twenty by day. We thought it compared pretty favourably with our own radios or the GPO!

On Friday 29 November we crossed the Equator. At lunchtime we held a small ceremony and drank a few toasts to mark the reaching of this epic point in our journey. That night we camped in a small clearing amongst some limestone outcrops. Nearby the jungle contained old plantations, and wild lemons were plentiful. There were also some interesting caves in the area; in one we found a great many initials which, according to local legends, included some carved by H. M. Stanley himself! Whilst studying Stanley's map at this point I noticed that he marked a large river coming in from the west which he called the Wakuti. However, I could find no trace of this and assume that it was a confusion with the Lomami which in fact was running parallel to us.

From ahead the recce reports of the Stanley Falls were good and there seemed to be no great problem. Having met Bill Coleridge's FST in Kisangani, John Strugnal, the manager of a local brewery, had kindly come out to greet us by road with a large quantity of his products. The party that ensued was one of those memorable evenings which often happen on an expedition and put us in a good mood to meet the final cataract of the Stanley Falls next day. It was right in front of the city of Kisangani (formerly Stanleyville). Here, thousands of people crowded on to the bank to cheer the fleet through. As each boat slipped over the six-foot drop into the heaving waves, a great cry went up from the shore.

'*Mobutu oyeah*,' we shouted over the loud-hailers.

'*Mobutu ooyeeah*,' echoed the people.

The Avons were hurled high by their impact with the waves, but the big rafts ambled through, all except *David Gestetner*, which delighted the onlookers by demolishing one of the fifteen-foot-high fish traps in mid-river. It was a great day for the expedition; we had now reached our half-way mark and John Strugnal's company kindly saw that the occasion was suitably marked when we came ashore.

In the town our signal section, who had flown ahead, had already set up a high radio mast and were in contact with the BBC in London. Sergeant Alan Cobb, our rear base radio operator in Kinshasa, had arranged the details and now we were to attempt the impossible: a link-up from the jungle to Broadcasting House. Early one morning I sat by the set as our signallers fiddled with the knobs and tried to beat the atmospheric conditions. At last there came the clear voice of someone at Catterick in Yorkshire.

'We're connecting you with the BBC now,' came the voice.

Various pips and squeaks followed and then a clearly audible woman telephonist in Broadcasting House was heard to say, 'I am sorry, dearie, but the number's engaged, you'll have to ring back.'

'Madam, I am in the middle of Africa,' I screamed into the handset.

'I can't help that, you'll still have to call back,' she said, and the line went dead!

Thus ended our attempt to communicate with the nation.

7. In the steps of Stanley

There is no fear that any other explorer will attempt what we have done in the cataract region. It would be insanity in a successor.

SIR HENRY STANLEY

Now 1000 miles of wide, slow-flowing river faced us. Stanley had fought great battles here, but the Zaïrois were overwhelming us with their traditional hospitality. It was as well that our relations with them were so good for Roger Chapman's life was suddenly at stake. He had been taken ill on the afternoon of Thursday 5 December with what was thought to be peritonitis, and Vyvyan Jones, one of our surgeons, was extremely worried about his condition.

'Are you really proposing to operate in this bush hospital?' I asked.

'Well, if I don't, I think he'll die,' he replied.

That night they gave Roger a spinal anaesthetic, which meant that, although he felt no pain, he remained conscious throughout the operation. Roger has a great Yorkshire wit and happened to notice that the two surgeons working on him were John Chapman-Smith, an eye surgeon from New Zealand, and Viv, a gynaecologist from Swindon. Apparently he remarked that he hoped they had reached a compromise before working on his middle!

However, by morning it was no laughing matter, for Roger was dying; the only chance of saving his life was to get him to a hospital where they could do a full laboratory investigation. The nearest was 1000 miles away in Kinshasa and although our Beaver could have covered the distance in two hops it was doubtful that there would be petrol at the end of the first 500 miles to get it the next. Even if there was, the chance of the patient surviving ten hours in a light aircraft in such a condition was remote.

At this point our guardian angel intervened and we managed

to get the assistance of the local Zaire general. He had been a military attaché in London and, apart from the fact that he spoke English, was clearly very fond of us. He therefore ordered the nearest airliner to land at Kisangani airfield, which it did. John Benham-Crosswell surrounded it with his 'mercenaries' and the French pilots put up their hands in surrender. However, John explained that this was not a *coup d'état* but simply a question of borrowing their aircraft for a few hours.

We loaded Roger, Viv Jones and Pam as the nurse on to the DC4 which took off for Kinshasa without delay. Roger was a great friend to all and we prayed hard that he would survive. It was fortunate that we had Pam with us because she had worked in the President's Clinic in Kinshasa and knew the people concerned. Therefore by sending her with Roger I felt happy that he would get the very best attention. Later, we heard that largely through the good efforts of Dr Bill Close, Pam's former boss and personal physician to the president, they had managed to save Roger's life, although not without a considerable struggle.

Meanwhile our fleet was once again under command of Mike Gambier. I planned to send the boats on whilst I moved east into the Ituri Forest through which Stanley had marched to rescue Emin Pasha in 1888. In this dark land live the Pygmies and the strange okapi, a type of giraffe with a backside like a zebra and a body similar to an antelope. It is peculiar to this part of Zaire and was only discovered around 1900. I was very keen to see the beast and badly wanted a few days away from the administrative nightmares so, accompanied by our photographers, I drove 350 miles towards the Mountains of the Moon. There we found two fine bulls in captivity and were privileged to meet the Pygmies who hunt these strange creatures for the government conservation department. In olden times the skin of the okapi was much sought after and was reserved for chiefs. Apparently it was supposed to bring an endless supply of pretty young girls to those who sat on it!

With the Pygmies we tried to find and film this rare animal. Marching deep into the twilight forest with our tiny near-naked friends, we searched for days, and although I was not lucky enough to see one myself, some members did get within twenty yards of them. The only creatures I met were far from gentle. On one of our sorties two Pygmies, Bongo, a Sandhurst-trained Zaire officer, Val Jones and I were moving along a narrow game-trail in thick jungle. Suddenly the leading Pygmy bounced past me like a little chocolate-coloured rubber ball; close behind him was Lieutenant Bongo, who yelled, 'Run!'; and behind him came a very angry jumbo, ears flapping and trunk raised. I leaped aside and just remembered to warn Val. Four irate elephants crashed past, scattering branches and leaves. They looked rather small and it was only later that I discovered they were the very dangerous pygmy variety that inhabit the Ituri Forest and are much feared by the locals. I couldn't imagine what had caused this unprovoked attack until I remembered that for some 3000 years Pygmies have been sticking arrows in jumbos' backsides.

The jungle hunts were arduous, but very exciting. To try to follow a Pygmy in the deep forest is not easy, especially if you are over four feet in height. The little warriors were quite superb hunters and very tough. Using their tiny bows they could transfix a cigarette packet at twenty paces with an arrow tipped with coagulent that would clot its victims blood in seconds. During the search a hunter accidentally shot himself in the foot with an arrow, but luckily it was not one of the poison-tipped variety; he went on to march seventeen miles with us that day!

When we returned to the village at night our hosts entertained us. We took turns at putting on dances and acts in our own language. Neither really understood the other but it was great fun. Ken Mason's songs made everyone hoot with laughter, Doug told Canadian jokes, Val did a Highland sword dance and Sam Qarau frightened the living daylights out of our tiny friends by drinking the contents of a paraffin lamp and then, with the aid of his Ronson lighter, blowing fire all around us.

From my point of view this short interlude was a chance to unwind. On an expedition there is rarely any rest for the leader and under extreme stress I find myself flitting between two characters: one, which is much stronger, tried hard to defeat the weaker. The only noticeable result of this struggle is that my whisky consumption goes up! However, when the weaker me begins to get the upper hand I find I may overreact to situations or exaggerate a problem. The difficulty is, as in war, to know which intelligence to reject and which to accept. I believe it is essential to keep one's mind as open as possible to avoid blocking out unpleasant information. This is why I enjoy having a small group of trusted aides in my Tac HQ. Peter, with his methodical and cautious approach, was an ideal intelligence officer whilst Pam, with her knowledge of Zaire and its people, was a splendid adviser on the local situation. Sam could be relied upon to make us laugh under the most adverse conditions.

Also working in the rain-forest was Ken Joysey, lean and enthusiastic director of the Cambridge University Zoological Museum, who was in hot pursuit of the West African otter shrew. There were no live specimens of this creature in captivity. Aided by the Pygmy bowmen, Gurkha soldiers and Sergeant Major Eddie McGee, Ken and our other zoologists probed deep into the Ituri. In the same party was Mike Gallagher, who had turned his attention to bat-catching and was producing a splendid collection for the British Museum.

Back on the river our botanists were hard at work, studying amongst other subjects the spread of a notorious water hyacinth. Outwardly it is a pretty violet and green plant that was introduced into the river from South America in 1954 as an ornament, but is now threatening to block parts of the great waterway.

On returning to our base in Kisangani I was able to review all the problems that faced the expedition whilst Mike Gambier sailed the fleet on towards Kinshasa. We faced a host of difficulties. Our casualties were growing alarmingly as malaria, in spite of regular doses of Paludrine, took its toll. Dysentery, hepatitis, sundry fevers and ear complaints were reducing our force daily. At one time it had been suggested that we had too many people on the expedition, but now I found myself with too few to carry out the necessary tasks that would get us to the Atlantic.

We were half-way through the expedition; the lack of money had left us terribly short of transport, which meant that I could not use all our personnel effectively. Also, some of the expedition scientists had understandably changed their plans once they saw the ground and now wanted to work in larger groups, which required fewer administrative personnel to support them than I had believed necessary when planning in Britain.

On the political front the Zaïrois were extremely sensitive and we had to be very careful not to say anything that would cause offence. At Kananga there seemed to be a running problem between the British and the other nationalities in the medical research teams. In minor disagreements the Zaïrois sided with the Belgians, with whom, of course, they had a common tongue. Unfortunately, I was too far away to intervene. It was incredible how the irrepressible Freddie Rodger managed to control and lead this group effectively in spite of this. The Zaïrois said he was 'another Stanley', because he made them work so hard!

However, there were no really serious personality problems in the expedition, perhaps because I was utterly ruthless. Indeed I cannot remember an expedition where there had been so few difficulties of this nature. The girls didn't create any real problems and were working very hard and well as members of the team. Indeed I believe that they were a cohesive element on the expedition. Whilst Pam was nursing Roger in Kinshasa Val had taken over as my PA and, with her Cordon Bleu training, was feeding us like fighting cocks.

The lack and delay of mail was causing concern, for in spite of the efforts of our postman, Corporal John Winterbottom, to get it speeded up, it always seemed to take a long time. Some mail appeared to be lost, but when you consider the length of our lines of communication it really was a miracle that we got any at all.

There was no real problem with stores except for the dire shortage of fuel and Land-Rover spares. Our transport, which had served us so faithfully, was now virtually worn out. Our preparation of the vehicles in Britain had not been all that I had wished, but the Fairey winches we were using were absolutely excellent and vital to the engineers. They got us out of many a tight corner.

The main reason for success on the river was the thorough reconnaissance that we were carrying out and the good equipment. The Sony video was especially valuable and I believe we must have been the first expedition ever to use this equipment in the field. It was showing itself to be soldier-proof and stood up to the heat and humidity extremely well.

We were very fortunate to have a cheery and intelligent Zaire newspaper reporter, Citoyen Mpoy, with us. He was a great help with our local public relations and wrote the most splendid reports about the good rapport between Britain and Zaire!

Although I consider that overall the discipline was fair I

tried to avoid the large towns wherever possible. It really would have been very useful to have had a regimental sergeant major to look after the number of soldiers. Officers tend to be rather hesitant about rebuking their men on expeditions, and I was constantly having to remind them about haircuts and turn-out. The problem is that with the scientists bearded and long-haired it was difficult to keep the soldiers to a normal military type of appearance. We had one or two minor discipline problems with both civilians and soldiers, but these were mostly caused by stupidity and thoughtlessness and were not serious.

The weather had been pretty good so far. We seemed to have dodged all the rain along the river and yet had managed to get just enough water to navigate over the rocks.

The roads were generally poor and seemed to be getting worse as we proceeded north, and I noticed that the jungle was encroaching on the country's road system at an alarming rate. The railway companies, on the other hand, were extremely helpful and did their utmost to look after us; and wherever we could find ferries, the local authorities were helpful. However, many of these had been destroyed in the civil war. Airstrips, on the other hand, were few and far between; many were overgrown but they were often still usable.

The animal hazards were mainly confined to the hippo, although we did see a few crocodiles and snakes were numerous. Mosquitoes were extremely bad in places and attacked without provocation, as did the tetse flies and other nuisances including scorpions.

On the whole the expedition was in good heart, although this was sometimes due to the supply of free beer! Several breweries along the river were about to be nationalized and were extremely generous. I foresaw problems with boredom as we moved over the long slow-flowing stretch that was to take us to the capital. Contrary to one report in the press, I thought morale was pretty good, and it was as well that it was, because ahead of us were the most difficult rapids yet.

Another problem was that, having left groups in Kisangani and Kananga, our communications were now stretched to over 1000 miles. The sets were simply not designed to cope with this, nor had we got enough radios to do it. Nevertheless, the Royal Signals team battled on bravely and somehow we always managed to get through.

The committee in London announced that in spite of our economies they had been forced to raise an overdraft and this we knew would take at least eighteen months of writing, lecturing and selling our philatelic souvenirs to repay, once we returned to Britain.

So the whole expedition moved slowly on towards the Atlantic. The fleet were moving faster on the river than I had anticipated; in the end, our Tac HQ had to fly ahead to Kinshasa by civil airliner and then back in the Beaver to join them. This I did on 17 December. When Pam and I landed at Mbandaka, we found the expedition had been royally entertained by personnel of the Wimpey Company. Alas, we had arrived too late for the party, but the recce section was waiting to take us forward to the giant inflatables, now motoring fast towards the west.

Neither Pam nor I felt particularly well and on the following morning I awoke with a mild fever, feeling very sleepy indeed. I had intended to hold a conference of captains on the flagship, but the river was terribly choppy, with two-foot-high waves making progress slower than usual. We were constantly soaked with water and therefore the conference had to be postponed. So I spent most of the day discussing our future moves with Mike Gambier. The one great advantage of having an able second-in-command, which I had learnt from my experiences in the Darien Gap, was that you could bring him in to take over so that you could move all over the expedition and find out what was going on.

For two or three days my fever ebbed and flowed and I didn't think too much of it. Indeed I was more worried and frustrated because our radio communications were made difficult by constant interference from a Chinese station operating from the Congo Republic on the north bank of the river. Then, on Saturday 21 December, I decided to move ahead with Alun Davies's recce boat to arrive in the capital ahead of the fleet. At Kinshasa I went straight up to Bill Close's house to see Roger Chapman who was then convalescing. Bill gave me a funny look and asked if I felt ill. 'A little hot,' I replied. He took my temperature, which was 104.5°F! Unemotionally he informed me that I had a variety of malaria and in a flash injected me. In spite of feeling reasonably normal I found myself rushed back to the newly established Tac HQ in the town where Adrianne and Val swabbed me down with ice bags, stark naked! It did the trick, for next day I was able to rise and greet the fleet when they came in to a tremendous welcome.

Christmas never feels quite the same in the tropics but the European families there threw open their houses and did their utmost to entertain us. It was our only rest in four months. Our sick were put into hospital and now we prepared to tackle the real horrors that lay ahead.

Whilst the boats were refitted for the battle with the great rapids of the Livingstone Falls, members managed to relax. Richard Dorman, a rather wild ensign in the Irish Guards, caused a great stir by hurling himself fully dressed into the swimming bath of the Intercontinental Hotel, complete with a packet of soap powder, to get an instant bubble bath which filled the entire pool! But at Tac HQ, now comfortably ensconced in a large flat in the city, the work went on.

The complete New Zealand jetboat team had arrived and informed me that they had not a great deal of time left. They were very experienced river-runners and had already done an excellent reconnaissance for us of the Livingstone Falls, which proved extremely useful in planning this last phase. Long discussions went on far into the night. There were a number of problems over film copyright and so on to be reconciled. Many of these had been brought about because the original company with whom all the negotiations had been carried out relating to the jets had now ceased to have any interest in the matter and I was therefore discussing details with the parent company from New Zealand and having to start from square one.

Captain Nigel Warren of the Gurkhas had been left with his FST at Kisangani to support the scientists working in that area and eventually withdraw them to the capital. Freddy was still at Kananga with his medical research team and contact with him was extremely difficult. But my diary for Tuesday 24 December read as follows:

> Christmas Eve. Val Jones* better this morning. Boat preparations continue and I was able to visit most outlying units including our radio station at the Calico Printers Association Factory. Communications to Kisangani are good. Spoke to Nigel Warren regarding medical problems and my concern for the rise in malaria casualties. Bill Close has advised me that we should change from Paludrine to Nivaquine. Local doctors believe this

* She had fallen sick having nursed me back to health.

is answer to the particular brand of malaria found in Zaire. Am unable to get through to Freddy Rodger to confirm that he agrees.

Friends from Britain, the Oatens,* arrived in time to join us for the expedition Christmas dinner. This had been laid on at the American School and was quite excellent. Jim Masters and his boys had done most of the cooking and everyone in good heart. ZLOs also attended. Spent a short time at Bill Close's house visiting Roger Chapman and returned in time for midnight mass, conducted by our chaplain, Basil Pratt. There were forty-one communicants and Basil had to use brandy and Christmas cake as wine and bread absent. Sang carols round fire afterwards.

Following my bout of malaria I was also struck with some pretty uncomfortable dysentery, but by New Year's Day I was fit again, the boats had been made ready, the engines tested, the crews briefed and a great crowd gathered on the Island of Mimosa near the capital to watch our fight with Kinsuka, first

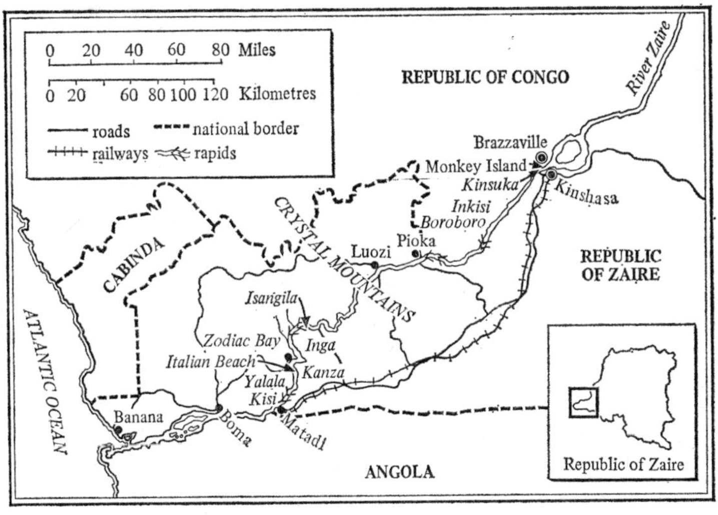

Livingstone Falls

of the thirty-two cataracts of the Livingstone Falls that cover more than 200 miles between Kinshasa and the Atlantic. Assisting us on much of the stretch were the two Hamilton water jetboats. They had been designed in New Zealand and built in Britain. These 220 horsepower, fast and highly

* Richard and Merrell, keen supporters of ZRE, had flown out especially to see us.

manoeuvrable craft were to be a vital part of the forthcoming operation.

At 1100 hours *La Vision* passed easily through the narrows where the river had now been constricted from something like nine miles wide to one mile across. Running down a smooth tongue of water, the inflatables skirted the line of tossing twenty-foot waves that rose and fell in the centre of the river. Acting as rescue boats the jetcraft lay in the lee of weed-covered boulders. Gerry Pass and Eric Rankin, the Survival–Anglia television team, had been positioned on one of these tiny islands to get a really first-rate shot of the drama, which they did when *David Gestetner* appeared with her white ensign fluttering. On the shore an elderly English lady missionary, overcome with emotion, is said to have burst into tears and then fainted at the sight. However, I put this down to the fact that the *Gestetner*'s crew were Royal Marines!

As the boat crossed the first fall, her stern engine struck a submerged rock which hurled it upwards off its wooden transom. The flaying propeller sliced through the neoprene fabric of the stern compartment, which deflated immediately. Aboard the jet we could not understand the cause of the trouble, but we could see the great raft was being swept out of control into the angry wave towers that we knew must be avoided at all costs. In a second Jon Hamilton, our skipper, had opened the throttle and driven the eighteen-foot boat straight into the pounding mounds of coffee-coloured water.

I could see Mike Gambier in the water; his white crash helmet and red life-jacket showing clearly, he bobbed amongst the flying spray. Our sister jet, driven by Ralph Brown, was already making for him with a scramble-net down the side. Lieutenant Nigel Armitage-Smith was standing by to pull him in. The deafening roar of water and engines drowned all commands. Everyone was acting instinctively now. *David Gestetner*'s skipper was trying to pass us a line, his face contorted as he yelled against the din.

Suddenly I heard Ken Mason yell, 'Watch out!' I looked up and saw an enormous wave had flung the crippled *Gestetner* forward and upward, straight towards us. For a moment she towered above, riding a fearsome wall of falling white water, and then came crashing down with a great 'ponk' right across us. For a second we were locked together in the tempest, but then we managed to wriggle from beneath and circle our quarry once again. This time we succeeded in taking the line and were soon dragging the craft like a stricken whale towards Monkey Island, where we managed to do the necessary emergency repairs. In fact, we were probably the first men ever to reach this large jungle-covered island, isolated in the middle of the rapids.

The next day, with all well again, we set off downriver. Rapid followed rapid as we cautiously felt our way through the treacherous waters that gurgled and swirled between the banks of black rock. To get the necessary supplies into the boats meant relays of overland teams working outwards from the capital in our very tired Land-Rovers and a few Toyota trucks that had been kindly lent to us. Wildlife was not much in evidence but on 2 January we did come across some islands literally alive with huge bats. There were thousands of them festooning the trees, and when I fired a flare from my signal pistol, the hideous creatures took off and showered us with their excreta. It is interesting that Stanley reported great flocks of birds in this area; I think that in fact he saw these colonies of bats. They must have had a twelve-inch wing span, and were obviously of value to the Zaïrois because we could see nets set up on tall poles at the side of the river to catch them.

In the days that followed we shot more rapids and avoided the most ferocious waves and water I've ever met. For each the drill was the same: air reconnaissance by Beaver, then the jets would take the skippers ahead to examine the heaving inconsistent flood and the swirling whirlpools that went up to thirty yards across. On either side vertical cliffs of red rock rose for hundreds of feet and fish eagles shrieked their yodelling cries as we passed. Meanwhile, our support teams worked day and night to get fuel and supplies into us over the deeply rutted tracks. In my log for Friday 3 January I recorded a typical day's sailing:

> Major rapids navigated were Inkisi and then the dreaded Borboro. Later we navigated an unnamed rapid which was not too severe. The river continues to drop and has fallen approximately 30 centimetres in twenty-four hours. Borboro was the most formidable rapid we have yet tackled. I did not dare to take the Avon S400s through manned and so ordered them to be towed by jets into centre of current and released without crews. This did not work as there is such a strong counter-current going upstream that they were continuously driven back, but, after some skilful

manoeuvring, we got them through. Went through myself in Jet 1 with Tac HQ; waves enormous, about nine metres high. Just as we left rapid a great boiling mass of water erupted with a deep rumbling sound right beside us; it was some two metres in height. When it subsided the water began to spin wildly and as it accelerated a vortex appeared in the centre and I gazed down into a horrific whirlpool some thirty metres across and three metres deep in the centre. The river around us had gone mad, waves breaking, rocks flashing by and all the 220 horsepower of the jet's engine were called upon to drag us from the grip of this revolving cavern. As we left it the hole closed up again and the surface became a sheet of fast-moving water. Similarly, another giant whirlpool appeared on our right and another ahead. The river was wild and it was almost as if some unseen force was trying to pluck us downwards.

On 6 January we reached Isangila, the falls that had forced Stanley to abandon his boats and march over the mountains to the sea. Here I decided reluctantly to move the giant rafts overland as far as the Yalala Falls, leaving the jets and the Avon dinghies to tackle the ferocious stream alone. The giant craft simply hadn't got the power to manoeuvre in these rushing currents and boiling water. In no time, one of the dinghies was ripped open from stem to stern on razor-sharp rocks and Jim Masters was injured. That night it took 900 stitches and a gallon of Araldite adhesive to repair the damaged boat. Jim drank a little J & B and recovered!

It was late afternoon when our jets entered the relatively clear passage that would take us through the terrible Isangila cataract. We were half-way down when I saw two gigantic waves converging on our bows. With a crash they struck simultaneously, hurling the 3000-pound boat upwards. I fell across Jon Hamilton, knocking him momentarily from the wheel, and out of the corner of my eye I saw Pam almost go over the side. Then as we hit the water again there was another huge wave towering ahead of us. For a moment I thought we were done for. It was a monster. The wall of water smashed over us blotting out the daylight; somehow we were still afloat. There was a strange silence; the engine had died. Ahead a line of black rocks rose like dragon's teeth on the lip of a fall and we were being swept straight towards them. Jon tried desperately to start the engine, his face creased with concern. Fortunately on the third attempt it fired. It only stuttered for a minute, but it was long enough for us to get into an eddy behind a huge boulder, where we could hold position whilst the electric bilge pumps baled us out.

Finally even the jets were halted by shallows and reefs at the Inga Rapid, but with two more short portages and some excellent warping with long ropes, we got the amazing Avon recce boats through to the foot of the biggest obstacle in the entire river, Yalala. A mile of water boiling over terraces and through jagged rocks at frightening speed greeted us. Meanwhile our giant rafts had been carried by a Zaire army lorry to within two miles of the river. Here we regrouped. Some of us had marched over the crystal mountains just as Stanley's men had done. We experienced the same elephant grass, endless rolling hills, ridges and sharp, suet-coloured quartz rocks underfoot that give these highlands its name. We too stumbled and fell on the slippery boulders at the river's edge. Ken Mason suffered a badly ripped arm and I injured my back. Porters, descendants of the people who had helped Stanley, assisted us.

At last we all came to the Yalala Falls, where the sappers were already clearing a way for us to carry the giant boats down to the river. For three days we toiled in the blistering heat with pick, spade and crowbar, and even some highly unstable dynamite, to clear the boulders and get the giant rafts to the water. Supporting us during this operation was our American officer, Captain Tom Mabe. Tom and his colleague, Sergeant John Connor, had come with us throughout the journey. Both were in the U S Special Forces and were useful members of our team, although I fear at times we must have driven them mad. Tom had managed to get hold of the explosive, but it was delivered at the Inga dam construction site and had to be driven to the river over a bumpy track.

It was late at night when Pam, Ken and I set out in a Land-Rover with at least two broken springs. In the back were large boxes of sticky, sweating dynamite and one crate of whisky. The vehicle lights didn't work particularly well and as we motored along the rutted road in the night, Ken began to ask about the dangers of premature initiation. We soon convinced him that our journey was likened to that shown so graphically in the film, *The Wages of Fear*.

'Oh my God,' he said, seizing a bottle of J&B from the back and clutching it between his legs.

'What on earth are you doing?' asked Pam.

'Well, I may as well get drunk and protect my courting

tackle at the same time,' rejoined our jovial photographer as we bounced along with our lethal cargo. The nervous tension made us roar with laughter and swig deep gulps of the bottle.

Pam at this point looked very much like a boy, with her hair covered in mud and her shirt in grease. In fact some Italian engineers whom we had met had referred to her as 'Fred the mechanic' and I don't think they really understood that she was a girl. Earlier in the expedition a chief had greeted her with '*Bonjour, monsieur*', but her confidence was restored when we discovered he was almost blind!

Finally, with sixty porters beneath each huge boat, we moved them like giant caterpillars down a 1000-foot slope to the river. Here we joined up with the Avon dinghies that had been portaged or controlled by lines through the surging white water towards us. Now only three rapids barred our way to the sea, but with up to sixteen million gallons per second pouring through a gorge which had narrowed the river to a bare 400 yards, the power can be imagined. Indeed the depth here was probably about 140 feet at high water. The river seemed to be alive with great boiling bubbles rushing up from the depths and erupting on the surface. Then as quickly as they came they were replaced by whirlpools and swirling currents.

Our porters, many of them Angolan refugees and some almost certainly Freedom Fighters, came with gifts of sugar-cane wine and fruit to see us off, but the river was not going to let us get away unscathed yet.

In the final rapid, *La Vision*, my flagship, was momentarily trapped in a whirlpool, like a cork in a wash tub, being bent downwards and spun round and round with engines screaming. Before I could stop them coming down Alun Davies's Avon was capsized by a fifteen-foot wave. The upturned boat with its crew of three clinging to it was swept towards a yawning whirlpool. The jets at this point had been sent back to Kinshasa, and from where I was situated 1000 yards down-river, I couldn't see what had happened. However the following recce boat saw the accident and its skipper, Neil Rickards, a Royal Marine corporal, decided to have a go. Taking his own small craft through the mountains of tossing water, he managed to get right into the whirlpool and circle around inside it, rather like a motor-cyclist in a 'wall of death' at a fairground. In the centre of this swirling mass he could see Alun's capsized Avon with its crew of three still clinging on frantically to the lifeline. Eventually, by going the same way that the water was revolving, Neil managed to get his craft alongside the stricken boat so that Bob Powell and Somue, one of the ZLOs, could pull the three men to safety. Then he circled up again in the same direction that the water was turning and out of the top. As they left he looked back and was just in time to see the upturned craft disappear down the vortex. Downriver, I was surprised a few moments later when the capsized boat bobbed up from the river bed beside me. The engine was smashed to pieces, the floorboards wrecked and there appeared to be no survivors. But the crew had all been saved thanks to Neil's courage and skill, for which he was later awarded the Queen's Gallantry Medal and made one of Britain's 'Men of the Year'.

Two days later we reached the little seaport of Banana and at dusk our strange fleet, which had set out almost four months before in the centre of Africa, sailed into the setting sun. Basil, in cassock and surplice, held an improvised cross and beneath the flags of the nations represented in our team, he conducted a simple service. Under our hulls the water heaved gently. Strangely, it no longer tugged and pulled at us; there was no current, for we were now in the Atlantic.

There had been many difficulties in the years that it had taken to plan and execute this expedition. Manpower had been extremely hard to find, money was almost non-existent and we had a long struggle in the early days persuading our Zaire friends that we were not a bunch of mercenaries. However in the end it had all been overcome and we had managed to prove Stanley wrong; although perhaps we had been insane to challenge this giant amongst rivers. Stanley, and what he had accomplished, had always been in our minds. In fact I don't think we ever forgot him and were full of admiration for what he and his force had taken 999 days to do when they had crossed Africa from coast to coast and come out with only 115 survivors of the 350 who had set out almost three years before. No one could appreciate what this remarkable boy from the workhouse at St Aspeth had achieved better than ourselves.

On return to Kinshasa we were privileged to be invited to the Presidency. There we met and talked with President Mobutu about the problems that his country faces. We were able to thank him for the considerable hospitality and kindness that we had received in his land. All he asked of us was that on our return home we should tell people of his hospitality and do what we could to help them to understand Zaire and his difficulties. This I gladly agreed to do, because on no previous expedition had we been received with such wonderful treatment from a ruler, government and people of a country which had not always had much to thank white men for.

Above all we had had a highly flexible plan. Naturally there had been tensions and there had been the usual vying between science and adventure, but it had worked and that was what counted. Now, when it was all over, there were bound to be those who would knock our success, but I have always found this is largely out of jealousy. I believe we succeeded because of our careful preparation, which had been carried out over a period of four years before we arrived with the main body in Zaire. The logistic support group had achieved an administrative miracle and how our doctors had kept us all so fit was beyond me. In fact, although over half of us did become casualties at one time or another, no one died.

We had a wonderful team. There were the young who had been brought up on the traditions of Outward Bound and the excellent junior NCOs who had had to take on enormous responsibility, often when they were completely out of contact with me and what was going on; but there were also fine civilian leaders as well. Naturally people occasionally wanted to scratch out my eyes, but I have always accepted full responsibility on an expedition for everything that goes wrong and I expect people to grumble at me rather than at each other. This helps to keep the team together. Lastly, of course, our equipment had been magnificent. The Beaver aircraft and some of the innovations of the twentieth century had all worked, but the one piece of kit I shall never forget were the giant inflatable boats that had wobbled their way all those thousands of miles across Africa. And it was primarily because of them that the expedition was later to be awarded the Segrave Trophy for courage, initiative, skill and imagination in pioneering new forms of transport. One of the previous winning craft had been Concorde; however, on at least one occasion we had managed twelve miles per hour with the wind behind us!

Of course the final measure of our success will be in the scientific results, which we hope will follow on and be of real value to the world, Africa and, in particular, the people of Zaire. I am not a scientist but simply, as a Royal Engineer, an 'obstacle-breaker' whose job it was to launch and sustain the experts in their selected areas to the best of my ability. Even as I write it is too early to say exactly what our scientists did achieve. Certainly Freddie Rodger's team made important discoveries in the battle against river blindness and his own book tells of their results.

The botanists from Leeds University had worked on the relationship of certain plants to mineral deposits and their work could well have important implications for the developing nations.

Our study of the papyrus in Zaire may help the world to make use of this raw material for low-grade paper now that the production of newsprint from wood pulp has become so expensive. A means of clearing the river of the choking water hyacinth was suggested to President Mobutu during our final interview. Furthermore Professor Harold Woolhouse, our chief botanist, believed that with more research this protein-rich plant might be used as animal food.

It is hoped that Jeremy Mallinson's conservation-orientated work on the mountain gorilla will contribute to the protection of this rare beast and that Keith Banister's team's results will add considerably to man's knowledge of fish evolution.

The anthropologist and geologists certainly had a field-day, whilst Stephen Sutton's entomologists' work should be of real value in the future understanding of the composition, vertical distribution and richness of the insects of the rain-forest canopy.

After the expedition Harold Woolhouse kindly said, 'We could never have undertaken this without Army support.' However, I felt the operation was only possible because of the expertise, teamwork and mutual respect that the Scientific Exploration Society had built up between civilians and servicemen of many nations.

In short, I believe that the whole expedition* had been a worth-while project with a good mixture of science and adventure, showing that there are still plenty of people about with the same healthy contempt for difficulties and dangers as Stanley and Livingstone had one hundred years ago.

* The full story of ZRE is told in Richard Snailham's *A Giant among Rivers* (Hutchinson, 1976).

8. Temples, torrents and tigers

The ten-foot crocodile rose slowly from the shallow, muddy water and slid silently up the sand-bank. Fifty yards away, eight-year-old Victoria watched with interest as the reptile opened its long thin jaws and eyed her mother's behind thoughtfully. Judith was standing in a locally made dugout canoe, intent upon her fishing, when Victoria spoke.

'I've told you before not to interrupt me,' she scolded.

'But Mummy,' interjected our daughter, 'it's quite important.'

Judith was concentrating on the next cast. 'Just a moment,' she replied.

The crocodile, fortunately a relatively harmless fish-eating type, slithered back into the swirling water of the river.

'Now, darling, what do you want?'

'Oh, it was only a big crocodile right behind us,' said Victoria, 'but he's gone now.'

No one in the boat believed her, but sitting on the bank 200 yards away, Jim Edwards and I had seen the whole incident.

We were spending Christmas 1975 in the mountainous kingdom of Nepal, assessing the navigational possibilities of a little-known river and photographing rare big game in the jungle and swamps of the Chitwan Valley.

It all started when Jim, who had spent a short time at Victoria College, strolled into my office in Whitehall.

'I've got a river that I'd like to open up for tourism and local traffic,' he explained. 'It's pretty rough, a few rapids; but nothing compared with the Nile or the Zaire.'

'Where is it?' I asked, my interest immediately drawn from the mass of Army paperwork that littered my desk.

'It's called the Trisuli and it runs from Tibet to India, through Nepal.'

In preparation for Zaire, a Hamilton Jet is tested on the Solent. L to r: Nigel Armitage-Smith, Pam Baker, JB-S, Hamilton pilot

Lunch at Crocodile Pool on the Zaire River. L to r: JB-S, Eric Rankin (Survival-Anglia TV team), Pam Baker, local chief, Mike Rowlatt

Opposite above: A spot of bother on the Trusuli River, Nepal. The Avon appears to be under-inflated

Opposite below: George, a great Indian one-horned rhino at bay, Chitwan, Nepal

Right: Off on a camera hunt with one of Jim Edwards's gentle elephants. L to r: Emma, Kelvin Kent, JB–S, Victoria

Below: Bengal tiger, the great cat, near Tiger Tops Lodge

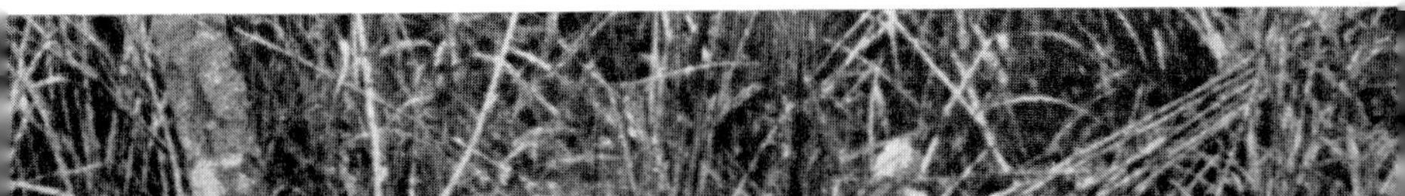

Victoria and Emma (right) during an elephant trek in the Nepal *terai*

JB-S demonstrates his faithful Philips memo-recorder to Cuna Indians on the site of New Edinburgh, Caledonia Bay 1976

Jim Edwards, safari expert extraordinary, explorer and hunter turned conservationist, lay back in the deep armchair. His off-white safari suit was in no way out of place as he sprawled, surrounded by the photos and maps of a score of expeditions that adorned the walls.

'By December the snows will have melted and the river will be low; you could have a good look at the rocks,' he continued. Jim has a flair for inspiring others to help in his projects and an impressive track record. These attributes, combined with good looks, a charming personality and his embarrassing generosity, make him a persuasive fellow.

'Haven't been at home for Christmas for . . .' I muttered.

'Bring the family, be my guests, it's great fun, we have a huge party at New Year,' interrupted my long-legged friend. 'I need someone with a sound knowledge of rivers to tell me if this idea is feasible.'

That night the Zaire River Expedition was to be presented with the Segrave Trophy at the Royal Automobile Club. 'Fine,' I said, 'but come to the RAC tonight and meet Judith.' He did, and easily won her wholehearted support.

With us in Nepal were Kelvin Kent and his wife, Jennifer, both of whom had been with me in the Darien Gap and were old friends of Jim's. Kelvin, then a Royal Signals major, was known for his expeditions in Nepal and had also served with the Gurkhas, but it was my first visit to this remote land.

We had arrived in the capital, Katmandu, in mid-December. The city nestles in a valley 4500 feet above sea level and above it the mountains seem to float, snow-capped, as part of the sky itself. But they are always there and it is impossible to forget them. Indeed they overshadow everything in Nepal.

The city is a mass of temples, covered with a profusion of carvings which one can spend hours examining! On the steps of these buildings there are market stalls upon which are piled vegetables and fruit in a kaleidoscope of colour. The Nepalese are engaging and attractive and the hill-people who come down daily to trade in the city seem to have permanent smiles radiating from their glowing, smooth faces. They accept foreigners as being a perfectly natural part of their scene and treated us with the greatest understanding, kindness and hospitality.

Our first task was to fit out the Avon inflatable craft with special wooden rowing frames. Because the only timber available was hardwood, I had to use this. However, in just under two days four local carpenters had constructed, with great expertise and skill, two excellent if somewhat heavy rowing frames. Certainly they had never built a boat or anything to do with one before! Our boat-yard was set up in Jim and Fjiola's garden overlooking the city, and whilst the girls explored Katmandu on hired bicycles, the men worked away in a temperature not unlike that of a midsummer's day in Surrey. In the early morning it is chilly and misty, rather as one would imagine the autumn in Britain, but around ten o'clock the sky clears and the towering mountain peaks appear as the valley floods with warm sunlight. Around the city the fields are cultivated into meticulous terraces and soon after dawn these are alive with people at work.

Nepal appeared to be made up of many and varied ethnic groups, wearing a colourful variety of clothing. There are refugees and traders from the surrounding countries including Tibet and Bhutan and also others from the lowland *terai* to the south. All these people come to the markets in the city to trade.

Nepalese are either Buddhists or Hindus, although Nepal is really a Hindu kingdom and it is the Hindu gods which are respected by all. However, it is the birth-place of Buddha and his influence is still considerable.

I felt we could not come to the Himalayas without seeing Mount Everest. So early one morning we boarded a Royal Nepal Airlines flight that takes tourists on one of the most fantastic sight-seeing trips in the world. Cruising at 20 000 feet, we winged eastward past the snow-capped peaks bathed in the pale morning sunlight. 'It looks like a great iced cake,' commented Emma as we rushed from window to window to get the best view. The panorama of desolate snow and ice inched past. Names like Melungtse, Chugimago, Karyolung, Gyachungkang, Namche-Bazar and Nuptse were given out over the aircraft intercom. And there behind Nuptse rose the highest wilderness of all – Everest, or Sagarmatha, as the Nepalese call the 'Queen of Mountains'.

It was hard to realize that we were looking at something almost six miles high; something of such a scale that it was unreal. 'How could mere man climb to the top of this?' I found myself asking, and yet over thirty climbers have reached the summit. I have to admire their courage, determination and tenacity and spare a thought for those who have died in this freezing, wind-swept wasteland. As we turned for home, I took one last look at Nuptse where my old friend Richard Summerton* and three friends had fallen to their deaths so recently. Their bodies are still there, part of the fearful Himalayas they loved. We all felt privileged to have glimpsed this world and, as a family, regard it as a special shared experience.

Back in Katmandu I recruited a crew. Jim's tough younger brother John would help us and Vince Martinelli, globe-trotting businessman from New York, would also give a hand. John knew Nepalese, so I made him the navigator, and as Vince was then a commodity-broker he became quartermaster.

The beautiful blonde Barbara Martinelli would add tone to the trip and my clutch of Blashford-Snells would frighten any hostile natives! Two smiling sherpas made up the party.

As soon as our boat was ready, we set out for the Trisuli River, which in December was dangerously low and fast. Roads are few and far between in Nepal and therefore it was of considerable interest to discover whether, with the use of new types of inflatable craft, we could navigate certain river systems and help to open up this interesting land. The bulbous grey Avon was the latest development of river-running boats, which we had first used in Ethiopia in 1968 and later on the mighty Zaire. Now the 'Professional', as we called it, was to be tried on the freezing cold, rushing waters of the Trisuli.

As the morning mist cleared John Edwards and I were able to carry out a reconnaissance of the first stretch of rapids and found that they were not unlike those that I have seen on the upper reaches of the Blue Nile. Whilst we did this poor Emma, now eleven but never a good car traveller, was sick and Victoria chatted up the sherpas. As a group of hillside children gathered to watch this scene there quickly grew a youthful understanding between these young from different worlds. They were fascinated by each others belongings and always compassionate; Emma was soon applying ointment to festering sores on a small child. Having selected a suitable spot we launched the Avon and, after a snack lunch, proceeded cautiously downriver.

The scenery was magnificent: brightly coloured birds darted amongst the scrub at the water's edge and the sun shone brightly on the polished white pebble banks. Everyone was in

* Captain Richard Summerton, Royal Engineers, had been with us in the Darien Gap.

a holiday mood and cameras clicked as we swept gently along. The rapids were sporting but not dangerous.

However, after a few miles I heard the warning boom of bigger water and pulled in for a foot recce.

Around a bend, beneath a steep cliff, the river narrowed and was suddenly whipped into a frenzy of white water. I decided that the girls should walk round whilst we negotiated it. It was as well they had left the boat for I made a complete nonsense about half-way down; the inflatable went out of control, and one of my oars jammed between two rocks and then, with a splintering crash, suddenly snapped. The end sprung back into my face with a sickening thud that pitched me backwards off the rowing frame. Momentarily stunned, I lay on my back in the bottom of the boat and watched the fleecy clouds rotating above. Suddenly a stopper wave crashed over us, half filling the Avon, and the freezing cold water brought me back to life with a jerk. As I struggled to regain my position and release one of the spare oars, I could see John and Vince fending off the black rocks with their paddles as we rode the foaming torrent.

Much of the force of the blow had been taken by my crash helmet and also by a new type of rather large Seiko chronometer on my wrist. Amazingly the chronometer still worked, but I had a beautiful black eye and a broken nose. As we came into the bank to bail out, blood poured from my nostrils and from a cut on the bridge.

'I must get a picture of that!' laughed Judith, ever sympathetic. 'Can't miss a chance for a spot of PR.'

'Lie still, Daddy,' hissed Victoria as, with a genuine concern on her face, she cleaned up my wound and applied a sticky plaster to the swelling snout.

The map wasn't a great help and although one or two of Jim Edwards's staff had been on the river at different times, the exact positions of the major cataracts were unknown.

To check our navigation we were using the original compass that had been carried by Stanley in his search for Dr Livingstone in 1871. This unique item had been presented to me just before leaving Britain and I had intended to hand it over to a friend at Heathrow. Unfortunately, due to the chaos of a fog-stricken airport, I was unable to meet up with him and so the compass went to the Himalayas.

The rapids got steadily worse as we moved downstream and

occasionally we saw bloated bodies floating past. These were not the victims of drowning, but the results of ritual burials that are regularly carried out along the banks of the river. Victoria found one or two particularly gruesome relics, including a very fresh skull, which she displayed with great pride!

The sun had left the steep-sided valley by mid-afternoon and there was a distinct chill in the air, so we pulled into a sandy beach for the night. In no time tents were up, dry clothes donned and the sherpas had killed, feathered and were roasting a chicken over a roaring wood fire. Emma helped me to filter river water with a Millbank bag whilst Victoria gave a hand with the supper.

The twilight was surprisingly long and we enjoyed one of those memorable scenes that I have been privileged to experience on several great rivers of the world – the ripple of water, calls of the night birds, crackle of the wood fire and a glass of my favourite Scotch; for Judith, remembering my love of J & B Rare, had a litre bottle to hand.

Sitting around the fire in our down anoraks we yarned, American, British and Nepalese voices gradually getting more slurred as the level in the J & B bottle receded. Next morning Barbara confessed she had had great difficulty in locating and getting into her sleeping bag. At dawn she awoke to find her legs in the arms of Vince's anorak!

On the second day the rapids were too bad for the girls to continue with us and therefore they returned to Katmandu by road in order to fly ahead to Nepal's unique jungle lodge, Tiger Tops, which was our expedition's destination.

Due to the severity of conditions, portage (one using a local bus along a riverside road) and warping were necessary from time to time; we met several formidable cataracts, comparable with some that I had seen on the Zaire. In one a wave swept me clean out of our Avon into the freezing water. Luckily Vince grabbed my foot and I soon found myself back aboard with teeth chattering! Foolishly I had not brought my rubber wetsuit with me and I recommend this as a vital item of equipment to anyone boating in Nepal. In another rapid we were swept up against a vertical wall of black rock and held there by the force of the water for long enough to be worried. On the nearby riverbank a ritual burial party, waiting patiently for an old man to die, stared in amazement.

It was mid-afternoon on the second day when we tried to

shoot through some foaming shallows. Suddenly, with a shriek of complaining fabric, we struck a boulder and became jammed. We swung broadside on to the river and at once green water poured into the craft.

'Quick,' I shouted to Vince, 'into the water, we've got to lift her over the rock.'

With commendable speed, the Wall Street broker was over the side, and together we heaved and struggled to lift the swamped boat.

'Stay on the oars,' I yelled at John.

Then, suddenly, we were free, the boat spinning wildly downstream through the tossing waves as Vince and I dragged ourselves aboard.

The two sherpas, who couldn't swim, had grinned bravely at all previous near-disasters. However, after this one they decided they had had enough. John argued, pleaded, begged, but it was to no avail; they reckoned we were insane and they were scared stiff. So, facing a long hard walk home to Katmandu, they left, saying as they went, 'Everest any time, but this is madness.'

The period from January to April is the dry season in the lowlands and therefore we were able to sleep on the sandy beaches alongside the river without tents; we had lightened our load by sending these back with the girls. Nevertheless a good warm sleeping bag was required and, personally, I wore every item of clothing I possessed inside it! At other periods the rivers would be swollen by monsoon rains and although I believe it would be possible to navigate the rapids more easily then, the purpose of our survey was to study the obstructions on the riverbed which are only visible at low levels.

However, because of the lack of water, the journey took twice as long as I had expected and by Christmas Eve we were almost out of rations. Our quartermaster examined the meagre resources and announced that our festive lunch would consist of a bottle of rum and six glucose biscuits! Whilst we were contemplating this miserable repast, three Gurung shepherds appeared from the hills with a bowl of cooked rice and some hot vegetable sauce. They were quite ignorant of the significance of shepherds arriving on Christmas Eve! Such is the hospitality of these humble folk that one man stayed with us all night to keep our fire going. By contrast the girls had spent Christmas Day on elephant rides into the jungle around Tiger

Tops and had caught their first sight of tiger taking bait at night.

Now, with our bellies full, we were able to face Christmas Day and a few more exciting rapids with greater confidence. We passed through an area of great scenic beauty at the bottom of a deep steep-sided gorge.

There was no road anywhere near here and we were very conscious that, if we lost the boat, it was a long, long walk.

We were now overdue and, having no radio, we couldn't even send Jim Edwards our position. So it was no surprise when we saw Dieter Plage's aircraft looking for us high above. Dieter was head of the Survival–Anglia film team in Nepal and was staying with Jim. It later transpired that they hadn't seen us and were worried.

We ourselves were beginning to notice the effects of the lack of sustenance. Crewing and rowing a white-water boat is hard work and, although we were all reasonably fit, the human body needs food. Even John, muscular and light, was finding it an effort to keep up the tiring bank recces.

Suffering from 'Katmandu trots,' Vince looked decidedly white about the gills. He didn't say much except an occasional 'Head for that sand-bank – I've GOT to stop.' Thank God for the Kukri rum! It's even better than Scotch for giving you energy.

There were occasional glimpses of red monkeys, deer and wildfowl before we finally reached our destination on Boxing Day. Suddenly the towering mountains and dark canyons were behind us and we floated out of the Himalayas on a wide slow-flowing flood to the beach at the little town of Narangayrh. Here began the *terai*, a narrow fertile area of jungle and swamp, in which is situated the unique Tiger Tops Lodge.

A great celebration awaited us. Jim, managing director of the project, had invited no fewer than 120 guests to join him over the New Year. They included scientists, soldiers, artists, mountaineers, conservationists and diplomats, including five ambassadors. All these people had come together to talk in an atmosphere of friendship because of their common love of wildlife and of a good party.

Jim's guests had reached Tiger Tops by bumpy Land-Rover rides or via a more comfortable forty-minute flight, skimming over the mountains from Katmandu to land on the grass airstrip at Merghauli. The airport 'taxis' are riding elephants who wait to transport new arrivals to the jungle lodge, which stands at the edge of the forest in the Royal Chitwan National Park. This is one of the best places in Asia to view many of the rare and endangered species of that part of the world. The *terai* or lowland jungle in which the park is found is less than one hundred miles south of Everest and Annapurna. It is around 500 feet above sea level and is in complete contrast to the northern part of the country. There are over 1000 square miles of virgin hardwood forest, one of the largest stretches anywhere in Asia. It is fringed by savannah and swamplands and the whole area is intersected by numerous tributaries to the Ganges.

The lodge consisted of a number of buildings on mahogany stilts. Rattan walls and thatched roofs helped them to blend into the environment. Shower baths were supplied with hot water from a system of solar heaters which had recently been installed. However, there were no generators, radios or noisy reminders of civilization. Lighting was by kerosene lamps and candles; and the centre of this jungle hamlet was a circular dining hall and bar built of local stone, with a neatly thatched roof. A gigantic fireplace stood in the middle of the room with its smoke rising vertically to the apex of the roof. Smiling, efficient Nepalese looked after us and carefully concealed hides enabled visitors to observe tiger and leopard, which come to baits after dark. At night these magnificent cats are illuminated by a pale yellow spotlight beam which, although insufficient to permit photography, does give the visitor a good view of these rare creatures. I couldn't help wondering about the possibilities of using image intensifiers to increase the viewing of these animals. However, from time to time the cats do come in daylight and during our visit the Survival–Anglia team was busy filming them.

A dozen well-trained, placid riding elephants are kept at Tiger Tops and it is by using these that Kelvin Kent, who had come down from Katmandu, Lisa, Chuck and I were able to make photographic forays into the dense jungle and areas of twenty-foot-high elephant grass that fringed the nearby Rapti River. The elephants are, of course, far less noisy than Land-Rovers and, because of their scent, are less likely to frighten away the game. Thus it is possible to approach animals in the jungle to within a matter of a few yards. At the nearby training camp, we examined the organization that makes all this possible. There were three men to each elephant, one being the *mahout* and the other two appointed to gather food for the great creatures and bath them in the river. I discovered that elephants adore bathing and therefore need water for this as well as for drinking. I also learnt that, on average, females are easier to train and handle than males. Their food consisted of masses of grass and large leaves with occasional titbits such as oranges or balls of rice cooked in saffron and wrapped in a leaf. I also discovered that an elephant has an interesting pace. Not all of them walk in the same way. Some bump along like a Land-Rover with a weak spring, whilst others glide much more smoothly.

Within only a few hundred yards of our camp, we were able to see both fish-eating crocodiles known as gharial and the more dangerous mugers, said to be man-eaters. In the forest we frequently saw deer, leopard and hundreds of monkeys. On one walk we found tracks of the Himalayan black bear that looked very fresh. Indeed they were, for Judith turned around and saw the creature right behind her in the trees!

However, the greatest excitement occurred in the swamps where the huge, two-ton, six-foot-high Indian one-horned rhinoceros lives. Once these creatures were even more common than the tiger, but today only about 1000 remain. Our first meeting was pretty dramatic. We were mounted on a frisky young elephant moving through long grass at the time when, without warning, the monster appeared only fifteen yards away. The first shock of a close-up view of one of these prehistoric-looking brutes is never to be forgotten. It really looks like something out of a Hollywood horror film and it took a few seconds before I could bring myself to start photographing it. Suddenly the great grey armour-plated beast tossed its head and came straight at us in a trundling charge. Luckily our elephant side-stepped at the last moment and then, to my astonishment, turned and charged the rhino! 'Isn't it fun, Daddy?' laughed Emma. But by this time my adrenalin was pumping round pretty fast and I was extremely relieved when the rhino eventually gave way!

However, those few days with the elephants left a lasting impression on me. Nowhere have I come across such amiable, sure-footed and easily controlled riding animals. They have an additional advantage over all others: their fifth limb, the trunk. With this they can help you to mount, clear a path through the forest wide enough for themselves and the *howdah* and feed from choice vegetation high in the trees. Their strength is enormous and if correctly applied can be used for a variety of engineer tasks. Man has Land-Rovers to cross deserts, snow-tracks to cross polar regions and hovercraft for swamps, but jungle is still an obstacle to mechanized transport and thus it is in these areas that so much scientific exploration remains to be done. Perhaps, as in Abyssinia with Lord Napier or in Burma with General Slim, the gentle jumbo may yet have another era ahead – and it doesn't use petrol!

There were more adventures to follow. One time a local boat broke down on the Rapti, stranding us all amongst a maze of sand-banks in the dark. Feeling our way through the shallow, fast-flowing water was no easy job. From time to time we plunged up to our necks on stepping into unseen holes in the riverbed; and Jim almost trod on a crocodile. Thus we were extremely glad to see the winking lights of a rescue party led by our Nepali friend, Nema Tenzing, cousin of the famous sherpa. Nema had missed us at last light and had immediately organized a search comparable with the most efficient mountain rescue operation I've ever seen. They cheered us with bottles of Kukri rum and so a very happy party returned to the small tented camp where I spent several most enjoyable days writing my report.

This camp was a day's march from the main lodge and tigers are frequently seen here, yet they seem to ignore the visitors. Here the river is the Gandaki and has been joined by the waters of the Trisuli down which we had journeyed during the earlier part of the expedition. From the tented camp we spent several days fishing for a lively member of the carp family called mahseer, which had been known to reach up to fifty pounds.

There are also some fresh-water porpoises that are endemic to these waters and I was lucky to catch a glimpse of a school when paddling quietly in local dugout canoes.

In the forest a rare wild buffalo called gaur (pronounced gore) is occasionally seen and we had one moment of excitement when a small herd of much-respected wild cattle appeared fifty yards away. We were just getting worried when a small boy walked out of the grass and drove them off with a stick! The domestic and wild beasts look identical!

In this pleasant climate we were extremely fit and the

children only suffered a couple of minor tummy upsets, whilst a couple of ticks made a temporary home on Judith. These were speedily removed by an attractive American nurse named Linda, who, with her boyfriend, Dan, were frequent visitors to Tiger Tops. They knew the Martinellis and soon we all became good friends. Dan Osman, a surgeon from Miami, was a particularly interesting man and with his quiet, common-sense approach to life and medicine was just the sort of man that is needed as an expedition doctor. Relaxing around the fire at night we found ourselves discussing all the usual legends of exploration, the Bermuda Triangle, Fawcett's disappearance, Atlantis, the Loch Ness Monster and, of course, the Yeti. I've always been interested in the stories of the Yeti, ever since I first met Odette Tchernine,* one of the leading authorities on the subject.

'Have you seen those people up by the airstrip?' inquired Dan.

'What people?'

'Well, there's some guys with mighty odd toes,' explained the surgeon, telling us how he'd seen a group of locals with big toes that pointed inwards, in severe cases almost at right angles. Kelvin said he'd try to photograph them when he next went to the strip and we talked of other things.

As the expedition drew to a close, an extraordinary event took place. On the banks of a stream I saw a most unusual set of footprints. They were rather like a monkey's with very big toes. They struck me as being very similar to the photographs I had seen of supposed Yeti tracks. However, in this case the cause was no hairy ape-like creature, but a smiling holy man with a pompom hairdo and deformed feet! In fact, just as Dan had said, his toes stuck out at angles and the feet were wider than usual. Apparently such mutations are fairly common in Nepal and, like those of the Yeti, the feet are described by local people as pointing backwards; however, it is in fact the big toe that points sideways. I feel that this deformity may well be a possible cause of many of the tales of Yeti tracks – there are plenty of gurus and Nepalese quite capable of walking around barefoot in the snow at high altitudes. Indeed, Sir Edmund Hillary shows a most interesting picture of a similar pair of feet in his book, *Nothing Venture, Nothing Win* (Hodder & Stoughton, 1974).

* Her book, *The Yeti*, was published in 1970 by Neville Spearman.

But did we stumble by chance on a reason for another expedition?

We completed the trip with a quick visit to Dharan, the British Army's Gurkha depot in eastern Nepal. Here Peter Macbeth, my best man, was the Commander Royal Engineers, responsible for a vast amount of work with a handful of dedicated sappers. Peter and his wife Gillian took us on a picnic to see another giant river, the mighty Suncosi, tumbling down through the mountain gorges from the 'Roof of the World' – Tibet. Perhaps one day the development of our river-navigation techniques may allow us to utilize this waterway as a route through this difficult country. But after my experiences on the Trisuli I knew that we must somehow find a way of applying more power to a craft that remains portable. It may be that a shallow-draught, water-jet-engined inflatable is the answer. Back to the drawing board!

Thus ended an exciting, interesting and highly enjoyable expedition in a land of wonderfully friendly people. It may perhaps result in the movement of villagers and tourists along some of the fast-flowing Himalayan river systems by inflatable boat and, in addition, who knows, perhaps it could provide an interesting line of research into the mysteries of the Abominable Snowman!

Nema came to the airport and as we were about to leave, presented each of us with a traditional *khadda*, a farewell scarf to give us a safe journey. We shall never forget the wonderful kindness and hospitality shown to us by the Nepalese that made it a most enjoyable expedition and the finest family holiday I have ever had.

9. The Americas again

Wallowing in my hotel suite bath with a tumbler of iced whisky close to hand, the thunder of the mighty Zaire and the hazards of exploration were forgotten. Then the phone buzzed. I let it buzz, but it persisted, so with an oath I rose and staggered forth, dripping wet.

A prominent part of my anatomy touched the door handle and I shot upwards like an Apollo rocket. In best Hollywood style, it was a blonde at the end of the line.

'What's wrong with you?' Pam asked innocently.

'This place is booby-trapped,' I groaned.

'Oh!' she said. 'That explains why Derek Jackson is lying stunned in the corridor.'

We had discovered the deadly static electricity for which that hotel is infamous.

However, a crate of J & B arrived with the compliments of the Paddington Corporation in time to revive us and Richard Oaten suggested lobsters for dinner at a favourite restaurant, the Palm, on Second Avenue. It was a splendid meal but, alas, when Richard, then a mere sixteen stone, rose to leave he discovered too late that the proprietor had moved the exit since his last visit. With a crash the fibre-board wall collapsed under him and we strolled over the wreckage into the street followed by a torrent of Italian curses.

Thus began one of our early pilgrimages to New York. Following the success of the Zaire River Expedition, Pam, Derek, Richard and I were there to give illustrated lectures or presentations.

Members of expeditions backed by the Scientific Exploration Society pay great attention to their audiovisual work and to present a really top-rate show takes considerable careful preparation. For at least two years after every expedition we usually tour schools and universities in Europe and the USA, telling them the story of the ventures. Indeed, much of our effort is aimed at youth, in the hope that young people will follow in our footsteps to carry on the work when we are no more.

Since 1969 the Explorers Club and the Scientific Exploration Society have co-operated, and, though the efforts of Mr Walter Annenberg (then the American ambassador in London), and a US banker, Norman Staples, the two organizations came together in Britain on a number of occasions. Thus our party had flown over to New York for the Explorers Club's annual dinner in 1975 where we were joined by two American members of the expedition. Tom Mabe and John Connor, resplendent in their US Army 'blues', flew in from Fort Bragg. Booking in at the hotel, we were contacted by Marie Roy, Russell Gurnee, Norman Staples, all of the Explorers Club, and also Ralph Barnett, chairman of the board of the Gestetner Corporation in the United States. The enthusiasm and friendliness of our hosts and sponsors struck us immediately.

Next morning I lodged a bottle of Scotch in the members' cupboard at the Explorers Club and we prepared our slides and film for the showing at the annual dinner. By early afternoon the level in the bottle had dropped and all was ready for the night. We just had time for a ten-minute TV interview before the dinner. Meanwhile, back at the hotel, Vince Martinelli was dangling beneath a huge balloon, Alec Staples was chatting up an attractive South American lady explorer and his father was smiling confidently (about the forthcoming dinner). The rest of the SES party were still leaping up and down on the end of the door handles.

I was honoured to sit between the famous Air Force general, James Doolittle, and Everest climber Barry Bishop, so I certainly had a splendid evening. The Explorers Club dinner, with its exotic menu and overwhelming hospitality, is certainly an event to remember. The rest of the night was spent in serious debate on scientific exploration in various establishments along Fifth Avenue.

Alas, all too soon we had to say farewell to our friends and it was after dark when we left JFK airport; two bottles of Pan Am's good claret later, London airport emerged out of the early morning mist. A quick dash in Pam's mini took us to Henley. Here on the Thames the *David Gestetner* was being relaunched at an old English pigeon pie and ale breakfast superbly organized by John Nunnelly. Amidst cheers, clicking of press cameras and clouds of coloured smoke, the giant inflatable set off downriver, not to explore the unknown reaches of the Thames or to shoot the rapids under Tower Bridge, but to advertise our forthcoming full-scale presentation at the Royal Albert Hall, which took place a few days later before an audience of over 3500, including members of the royal family, diplomats, service chiefs and heads of industry.

So through 1975 the hurly-burly of lecturing, film-editing and writing went on to raise the cash to pay for our Zaire exploration. By Christmas I was pretty exhausted and had gone on our family outing to Nepal, thinking that it would be my last expedition for at least eighteen months. However, a good fairy popped up and waved a magic wand, and thus in April we were off to the Americas again.

As so often happens, you reveal another tantalizing mystery whilst pursuing the main aim of an expedition and thus it was that, whilst crossing the infamous Darien Gap in 1972, I had heard of Caledonia Bay, the 'lost colony of the Scots'. Peter Marett, our thorough information officer, had drawn my attention to the story whilst we hacked our way through the claustrophobic rain-forest.

In the chronicle of Pedro Martín de Andleria, written in the early sixteenth century, the River Darien is mentioned as flowing into the Gulf of Uraba. Later the river changed its name to Atrato, but the area between Panama City and the mountains of Colombia became known as Darien. At about the same time the Spaniards called it Castilia del Oro – Golden Castile. It was so named for very good reasons; it can blame its troubled history on the fact that its jungle-covered land was rich with gold. Since 1501, when Rodrigo Bastidas became the first known traveller to visit the Darien, men have battled for the soft yellow metal. In 1502 when Columbus arrived he saw 'greater evidence of gold on the first two days than in four years in Hispaniola'. The Indians even wore solid gold breastplates, which they were quite happy to exchange for small bells or trinkets costing almost nothing.

It was to this area that William Paterson, an erratically brilliant Scot who helped to found the Bank of England, brought colonists from over the Atlantic. He called it 'this door of the seas, and the key of the Universe', and believed that he could make it a bridge between East and West. He proposed to build a port through which would pass some of the richest trade in the world. His concept was an excellent idea but, as events were to prove, the timing was wrong.

It was in July 1698 that five ships carrying 1200 people left Leith in Scotland and four months later dropped anchor in a natural harbour on the Darien coast which they named Caledonia Bay. It was sheltered from the ocean by a long, hilly peninsula. Soon after arriving, Paterson wrote:

> The land on the peninsula is extraordinary good, and full of stately trees fit for all uses, and full of pleasant birds, as is also the opposite shore, and hath several small springs which we hope will hold in the driest season. . . . our situation is in one of the best and most defensible harbours, perhaps, in the world. The country is healthful to a wonder, in so much as our own sick they were many when we arrived, are now generally cured. The country is exceedingly fertile and the weather temperate.

The Indians, too, were friendly, and soon found that they had nothing to fear from the good Scots. After two months of internal wrangling, they got down to building a settlement, which they named New Edinburgh. It was not the first European town seen in this area, for 181 years before, Balboa had been executed at Acla, said to be barely a stone's throw away; but now Acla had disappeared under the jungle. The Scots expected attacks by the Spanish and started to build a fort, but owing to lack of leadership it was never completed. The greatest danger, however, was from the English governors of Jamaica, Barbados and New York, who forbade English ships to trade with the new Scottish colony. The reason is uncertain, but it was probably pure jealousy of the Scots.

There was another problem. None of the five ships of the expedition could leave the harbour. They were unable to sail to windward and, at certain times of the year, the wind blew from the north-east, straight into the harbour mouth. Two ships did try to escape, but one was captured by the Spaniards when she ran aground and the other took a month to cover 120 miles, returning eventually to New Edinburgh. The result was that no provisions could be brought in. The outside world was as much use to the colonists as if they had been on the moon.

In April 1699 the rain started. Only then did Paterson realize why there were no white settlements between Portobello and Cartagena, for with the rain came the mosquito which, though he did not know it, carried yellow fever and malaria. After six months, one-quarter of the colonists had died.

> Our men did not only continue daily to grow more weakly and sickly, but more without hope of recovery, because about the latter end of the month of April, we found several species of the little provisions we had left in a manner utterly spoiled and rotten.

In June Paterson himself fell ill, and was carried aboard one of the ships, the *Unicorn*. To the other survivors this was the signal to abandon the colony. Four ships with hardly enough healthy men to crew them left the bay. The *Unicorn* and the *Caledonia* arrived at New York having lost 255 men. The *Endeavour* was abandoned at sea, while the *St Andrew* was chased by the Spanish fleet and 137 men perished. She eventually reached Jamaica with an army officer in command.

Of Paterson, when he reached New York, it was said, 'He looks more like a skeleton than a man. God grant he may recover . . . the grief has broke Mr Paterson's heart and brain, and now he is a child.'

The story of the colony did not end there. More ships sailed from Scotland. Only some arrived at Caledonia Bay, and they were met by a few survivors of the first expedition who had returned from New York. Different problems confronted the newcomers. Rumours of Spanish attack were common. Squabbling was continual, and no overall leader emerged until Captain Alexander Campbell of Fonab arrived. He immediately set out with 200 men and, with the help of friendly Indians, located, attacked and defeated an approaching Spanish force in the jungle. On returning to Caledonia Bay he found it blockaded by the enemy fleet, which then proceeded to disembark men on the flanks of the town. Campbell sent out scouts to check on their progress, but these were picked off by snipers in the thick forest. The rest withdrew hastily to the besieged settlement, where not only fever, but also a fire took its toll. The siege lasted for just over a month. The defenders seemed to have absolutely no chance of survival, but when it was least expected, the Spanish general offered astonishingly generous terms of peace. The Scots would be allowed fourteen days to stock their ships and to sail with the next favourable wind with all their guns and ammunition. Naturally enough the offer was accepted and on 12 April 1700 the last Scotsman left New

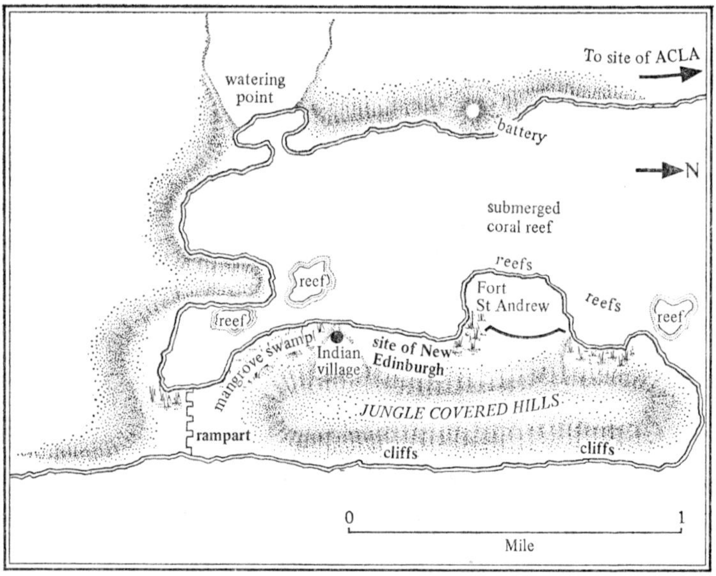

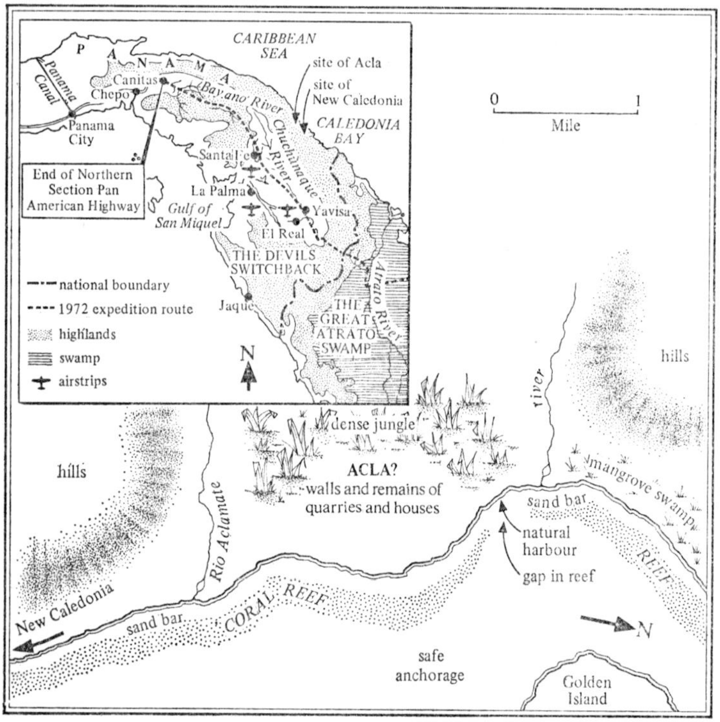

Top Site of lost colony of New Caledonia. *Below* Supposed site of lost city of Acla

Edinburgh. The Spaniards were left to reign supreme over the steaming isthmus.

So only three years after the Scots, in a wave of almost hysterical enthusiasm, had subscribed almost half their nation's capital to set up 'this noble undertaking', it had been crippled by the quarrelling of its leaders, deliberately opposed by the English Parliament whose king they had defied, and forced out by the Spanish. Nine ships of the company had been sunk or destroyed and over 2000 souls had perished on that fever-ridden coastline. It was a sad end to Scotland's last act of independence.

In 1972, whilst wrestling with the problems of the British Trans-Americas Expedition, Peter Marett and I flew along that coastline and, by using a map in John Prebble's outstanding book, *The Darien Disaster*, we found an area which looked very like the lost colony. A storm was raging and there was nowhere to land, but we were able to circle for fifteen minutes and take film and photographs of what I felt sure was the ill-fated Scots colony of 1699. During my journey through that awful forest I had often heard intriguing rumours about a lost tribe, said to be descended from the Scots, and also of the Spanish city of Acla from which Balboa had marched across the isthmus in 1513 to discover the Pacific. The mystery had intrigued me and I determined to return one day.

So in 1976 to investigate these mysteries I formed a reconnaissance expedition of three girls and seven men, which was backed by the Scientific Exploration Society and the Explorers Club. The members came from Britain, Panama and the USA. They were to include Vince Martinelli from New York who had been with me in Nepal and now came as quartermaster. Dr Dan Osman and his attractive girlfriend, Linda, whom we had also met in Nepal, would come from Miami as medical officer and nurse. A US Army NCO, Sergeant Mel Trafford, volunteered to be our driver, whilst the British contingent included a highly efficient PR executive, Ruth Mindel, who had joined our organization in London and now acted as general manager, treasurer and air adjutant. Andrew Mitchell, a light-hearted twenty-three-year-old zoologist from Jersey, became our chief scientist, whilst my ever-smiling aide Chris Sainsbury, recently returned from a voyage on a square rigger, was in charge of all sea movement, as well as being the photographer.

I wrote in advance to Dr Reina Torres De Arauz, the energetic director of Panama's Patrimonio Histórico, and she offered to help by providing an archaeologist who could also act as liaison officer. Meanwhile Mary Graham, an American doctor of Scots descent who was the society's local representative, kindly made preparations for our arrival and in no time our advance party was on the way to Panama City.

The horrors of a previous battle with the jungle were almost all forgotten. Indeed it really felt good to be going back to Darien and thankfully many old and valuable friends still remained from our last visit.

However, *en route* I had an assignment in New York; the 1976 Explorers Club annual dinner was to be entertained by a strange creature. Vince had telephoned me a few weeks earlier; he sounded excited.

'John, there's a guy over here with a live humanoid, says it comes from Zaire.'

'Have you seen it?' I said.

'Yeah! It's about four foot tall, one hundred and fifty pounds, kind of hairy body but with a more or less human face. It's pretty bald and the skin on the head is yellow, and what's more it walks upright all the time! Did you see anything like that in Zaire?'

'Certainly,' I replied. 'If it's got two pips on its shoulder I know just who it is, although I thought he was back with his regiment.'

'But John,' Vince insisted, 'I'm serious, some people claim it's a living Yeti and they say it comes from Zaire.'

Apparently a chromosome analysis of the creature had indicated that it was genetically abnormal. For some reason that I couldn't understand the beast had not then been fully examined by a qualified scientific team. Vince told me that the owners would be happy for me to inspect Oliver, as it was known, because of my knowledge of his alleged homeland.

'I'm no anthropologist,' I protested, but in the end agreed to meet the humanoid. Thus Jeremy Mallinson and Andrew Mitchell prepared me a brief so that when I flew to New York a few days later I was all set for the confrontation.

As our US Army friends had turned up in uniform the previous year I had been asked to attend the 1976 dinner in full Royal Engineer mess kit. At least there would be one Redcoat around in the Bicentennial year!

As I was dressing for the dinner, Vince phoned.

'John,' he groaned, 'I'm in a fix. That damned humanoid is fighting mad and they can't get it into its cage to put it on the light aircraft that's bringing it to New York.'

Apparently it had attacked its keeper and everyone else it could lay hands on. It looked as if the evening would be a flop; or a terrible disaster!

However, by the time we got into the hors d'oeuvres room we learned that Oliver, still in a frightful rage, had been boxed and was on his way. Vince, who was in charge of the humanoid's appearance, was still anxious as we sampled the dishes of peacock, llama, rattlesnake, dried fish lips, wild boar and something called *houma-houma-nuka-nuka-waka-walla*, which tasted like chicken.

We were seated and well into the main course when Oliver arrived. I was told that I might view the creature privately provided that I accepted full responsibility for its actions. After several false starts I was eventually permitted to go backstage and meet the keeper, a large South African attired in a green ringmaster's uniform.

'Now, you know the risk you're running,' he said, reaching for the bolts on the sturdy box.

Two sheriff's deputies who stood near by dropped their hands on to their revolvers. As the last bolt was drawn the door swung open and out popped the most extraordinary creature I've ever seen. Oliver was certainly ape-like and as he hopped up on a chair, he seemed to be grinning, although I fancied this was an expression of fear. Remembering my scientific briefing I asked if I might touch the beast. The keeper seized the length of chain that was attached to Oliver's neck and led him towards me. He walked upright with a shuffling gait and stretched out his great black hand. I took it in mine and immediately felt the power of its grip. Oliver studied me and I studied him. His eyes caught my miniature medals and for a moment I thought he would grab them, but instead he simply played with my hand and made a mewing sound, moving his lips as if he was trying to imitate human speech.

From the neck down he looked just like a large chimpanzee with a thin coat of hair. The hands and feet were certainly very ape-like, although I noticed that the knuckles were free of callouses. The head and face were most unusual. The skin was fair – a yellow colour, with very little hair. Indeed the creature had a bald, rather small head.

The mouth seemed much smaller and the jaws far less prominent than a chimp's. This feature tended to give it a human expression and I bent forward for a closer look. Oliver grinned and I saw that he was toothless.

'What happened to his teeth?' I asked.

'Oh! he got pyorrhoea so I had to pull them out,' replied the keeper. Perhaps this accounted for the flatness of the face.

Moving slowly, I eased my hand up until my fingers reached the hairy armpit, then withdrawing my hand, I smelt it. Oliver had little or no body odour. As he was alleged to have been in a rage that evening I found this hard to understand. When he shuffled away with his strange upright walk I pursed my lips and made several high-pitched squeaks. There was no reaction and I wondered if this might indicate a loss of high-tone hearing, possibly attributable to old age.

The dinner was ending and shortly Oliver must appear before the thousand or so members, so I had to ask my questions quickly.

'Whereabouts in Zaire did he come from?'

'Oh! On the Zaire River somewhere near Sierra Leone,' replied the South African gentleman.

I tried to conceal my incredulity and went on to inquire who had done the blood tests. A hospital that meant nothing to me was named and then the keeper said he really must leave me.

So, from the wings of the Waldorf Astoria ballroom stage I watched Oliver do his act. Led by his chain, he walked upright the whole time; his expression changed rarely, apart from an occasional grin. He gave a most convincing performance as a humanoid, but it was my feeling that he was probably an old, well-trained chimpanzee, possibly a mutant, who may have had some treatment to his face. I felt rather sorry for this extraordinary creature. The TV and radio pounced on me as I returned to Vince and Barbara at the table.

'What do you think, could it be the Yeti, did you see anything like that in Africa?' came the questions.

I explained I was no expert and admitted that I had not met anything like it before; but I rather doubted that it was the Yeti.

The next night, to maintain the tradition, our group dined at the Palm on Second Avenue. Our behaviour was exemplary and all went well until I was describing a pageant I had in mind, depicting the use of engines of war throughout the years. It was as I was demonstrating how burning peasants could be hurled over castle walls that my upflung hand caught a huge dish of hot french fries and scattered them all over the diners. I apologized profusely, especially to one lady with a plunging neckline who was clearly in some discomfort as a result of my careless gesture. We have not disturbed the peace of the Palm since then.

A few days later, whilst doing a radio show, I bumped into a colourful character named Tristan Jones. He is a Welsh seafarer of the old tradition; a lone sailor who has covered almost every stretch of water in the world. Tristan had even navigated rivers rising in the high Andes of South America with a clumsy sailing boat. As we left the studio we swopped yarns and talked of the many places where we had almost met each other.

'I'm just off to a place where I'm certain you haven't been,' I said.

'Where the hell is that?' my salty friend replied.

'Oh, it's a little-known bay called Punta Escoces,' I replied.

As we got into the lift he turned and winked. 'Was there last month, old fruit,' he grinned.

Of all the incredible coincidences I discovered that he had indeed only just come from Caledonia Bay. Furthermore, to our great interest, he told us that he had actually seen a tribe of primitive white people; rather short in stature, with red hair and blue eyes.

'Must be Scots, looked just as if they had come from Sauchiehall Street!' he joked. But he was quite serious about their existence. His words were still ringing in my ears three days later when I reached Panama.

10. Caledonia Bay

In Panama, Chris Sainsbury and Andrew had already done most of the preparation with the generous help of the British Ambassador, Mr Robert John, and our old friend Jack Davis.

I visited the Guardia Nacional and saw Colonel Flores, who had helped us previously. It was Easter and he regretted that all his men were on leave, so none could accompany us.

'You know our jungle well enough anyway,' grinned the colonel, indicating that he had no objection to my operating unescorted so close to the Colombian border.

True to her word, Dr Reina Torres De Arauz had maps and a young archaeologist ready, whilst the American, Dean Webster, an enthusiastic scholar of Panama's history, provided sketches of likely sites of Balboa's city of Acla. These, coupled with air photographs obtained by Andrew, were vital to our quest.

Meanwhile Ruth had gathered in an impressive stock of liquor and arranged an airlift to a grass landing-strip on an isolated islet about ten miles north of our target. The rest of our team arrived from New York and Miami and the hunt was on.

Winging away from the high-rise hotels of Panama City, we were soon over the dense jungle of the Darien Gap. Memories flooded back of those desperate days in 1972, when our column had struggled through the green twilight world beneath the tree tops. But now the track we had hacked so laboriously was a two-way vehicle highway with the greedy jungle cut back for fifty yards on either side. The brown earth road ran as straight as a sunbeam towards the far horizon. Where Ernie Durey and his sappers had rafted us across the fast-flowing Rio Bayano, there was now a steel bridge over a placid turquoise-blue lake, dotted with small islands and half-submerged trees. The long awaited Bayano Dam had been completed and already the rising waters were flooding back into the Cuna Indians' hunting grounds.

The little village of Torti had grown into a sprawling township as the highway engineers pressed on towards Santa Fe. I'd been told that the road was planned only as far as Yavisa and, doubtless, years of heated political discussion would take place before it was joined with the Colombian portion. Only then would the 17000-mile Pan-American Highway be complete.

Four thousand feet beneath us, the familiar, undulating green was slashed open by the dusty brown scar that disappeared into the purple foothills. Already the Pan-American Highway was seventy miles into the gap and the waters were rising in the Bayano Dam. Tree tops broke the spreading lake surface, their dying branches reaching out, finger-like, in a final protest against the flood that would soon engulf the traditional hunting grounds of the Cuna and the homes of the sloth, jaguar, tapir and a thousand other creatures of the forest. But Panama must have water and someone must pay the price.

'Took us six weeks to reach that village,' I shouted to Barbara and Linda, sitting behind me. The girls nodded their acknowledgement and peered down at the placid vegetation that looked so innocuous. Now the ground was rising up as we approached the Caribbean coast and a few miles ahead I could see the shimmering blue sea and the emerald isles of Mulatudo, Tubuala and Tupak. The villages, tightly packed huts crowded on coral outcrops, lay inside this protective barrier of swampy islands. Mulatudo airstrip had been built on the longest stretch of dry land and the pilot aimed the plane at its eastern end. Brilliant white egrets rose in alarm from the mangrove as we roared in and then with a bump and a thump we were down and taxi-ing towards Chris Sainsbury who, having arrived alone with the cargo three hours earlier, was somewhat relieved to see us!

'Welcome to Mulatudo,' he grinned, his fair skin already showing the effect of the glare. 'Actually I thought for a time that I'd got the wrong island, but I had all the liquor so I knew you'd find me!'

'Where are Andrew and Gricelio?' I asked.

'No sign,' said Chris.

'Probably been eaten,' remarked Ruth, who was still feeling the effects of the fifty-four ticks she'd collected on Barro Colorado island two days before. They'd been devils to remove and had defeated lighted cigarettes, salt and insect repellent.

Only vodka (Smirnoff's, of course), applied in an eye bath to the loathsome creatures, had made them release their grip. Perhaps that is the origin of the saying, 'As tight as a tick'.

It was strange that our advance party was not here to greet us. Only a handful of unsmiling Cuna Indians had appeared and, without orders from us, were already carrying all our worldly goods to the beach. Dan mentioned that because of the high Cuban population in his home-town, Miami, he had learnt some Spanish so that he could treat them. Thus he was quickly dispatched in a narrow sailing dugout to the nearest village.

'Make sure my camera case stays dry,' yelled Chris.

'Take care, honey,' urged Linda.

The doctor, in his new role of interpreter, looked decidedly uneasy and was already bailing the boat with a gourd. However, no sooner had he left when a motorboat appeared, bearing our wild-eyed zoologist, Andrew. A shock of tousled black hair flowed from beneath his army jungle hat, giving him the appearance of a Cuban revolutionary.

'Terribly sorry I'm late, spot of bother with the chief,' he explained.

'But I thought we had a letter from the government to him,' I replied.

'Yes, we did, but wrong chief. However, it's all right; Gricelio had a spare sheet of official paper and we borrowed a typewriter, produced a new letter, forged a good signature and here it is,' he panted. 'Now we've told the chief that you are our great leader and that the letter to him is only entrusted to you – so when you meet him, you can hand this over.'

So it was, a little time later, that I confronted the chief in the spacious village hall. Surrounded by his people, the wizened little man in a cowboy hat listened, whilst the local schoolmaster read aloud the official document. I sat, still wearing my freshly whitened pith helmet, looking as resolute, dignified and self-confident as possible, for I knew the Cuna of old. When the reading was over, I used the schoolmaster and Gricelio to explain in more detail what we were about. There were few questions and I sensed that we were not entirely welcome. However, the chief provided boats and boatmen to accompany us for the expedition (at an inflated price), and we wasted no time in getting under way.

'Did you see the albinos, John?' queried Dan, who had been

examining two or three of the fair-skinned, blond-haired Indians.

'Yes, they are reasonably common,' I replied.

'But there are so many, and they don't seem as severely affected by the sun as albinos usually are,' continued the doctor.

'Do you think they are lost Scots?' inquired Barbara, ever anxious about her ancestry.

The conversation ended as Vince, taking up his quartermaster's duties, got us all loading the boats. It was early afternoon as our flotilla of outboard-powered dugouts sped across the mirror-like waters between the islands, heading south-east to Punta Escoces, 'Scots Point'.

Canoes, expertly paddled by stocky Cuna girls in brilliant scarlet and yellow dresses and shawls, emerged from the coconut groves in the landscape that would rival any *National Geographic* spread. Gold nose-rings and chest discs flashed in the sun as their dusky brown arms worked in unison. Occasionally the light breeze lifted a shawl to reveal dark flashing eyes and strong mongol features.

The dugouts leaked and as we came out of the shelter of Golden Isle into the gentle swell, a wave or two slopped over the bow. However, this did not detract from the beauty of my first sea-level view of Punta Escoces or, as the Scots called it, New Caledonia. The leaning palms and golden beaches, the coral gardens and running surf, bright green hills and the shadowy mangrove at the far end of the inlet, all combined to make this place one of the most bewitching natural harbours I have ever seen.

Domitri, our leading boatman, suggested we base ourselves in some empty 'pueblos' in the Cuna village and we came ashore with a Panamanian flag flying. The huts were furnished with basic furniture, kitchenware and even a few *hamacas*, of the same type that had inspired Christopher Columbus's men to adopt this convenient sleeping arrangement.

The history of the area is fascinating and intrigued me. In 1503 Colombus arrived off the coast, seeking a way around the world, and although he knew it not, he was only forty miles from the Pacific, but it was four centuries later before the Panama Canal linked the oceans. Balboa's Acla must be somewhere in the nearby jungle and hopefully we'd find it. Sir Francis Drake is also thought to have used this hidden bay as a secret raiding base and to have named it Port Pheasant.

Perhaps his expert seamanship had enabled him to sail out against the contrary winds that had plagued the Scots captains.

I was acutely aware as I have never been before of the presence of the past.

During the dry season a small family of Cuna lived in the village to harvest the coconuts. Domitri agreed with a vocal lady that we should rent two of the houses and we moved in. By dusk Barbara had the kitchen set up, Ruth was happily surprised to find avocado pears were free, Andrew was in hot pursuit of the swarming blue land crabs that scuttled amongst the palms and Mel had recced the underwater obstacles near the beach. Gricelio was questioning the locals about artefacts and Dan had spotted another albino. The sun set in a blaze of orange behind the Darien Hills and, in the last rays, Chris filmed the Explorers Club flag, which barely moved in the humid evening air.

After supper I spread out the maps and air photographs and, fortified with a glass of lukewarm J & B, we planned the next day's exploration. Now we should know if all the research done by Reina Arauz and Dean Webster paid off.

Dawn came with heat, sand-flies and the good-humoured banter that characterizes an expedition. Having told everyone I expected them to rise at first light I'd slept until the sun was well up and received a good deal of well-deserved leg-pulling. However, a leader must have some perks! There seemed little doubt that the village was on the site of New Edinburgh. John Prebble's book gives a good description of the town and our archaeologist soon located evidence of foundations.

Our first task was to find Fort St Andrew. So leaving one party to examine the shoreline reefs, I took another through the coconut groves towards a promontory on which the old Scots maps showed the refuge. We found a stream of clear water running from the hills and I felt it should lead to our objective, but the vegetation grew thicker and the brook became a swamp, so moving inland again, I began to cut with my machete. Suddenly the ground dropped away steeply and I stumbled down into a shallow ravine. On either side the undergrowth fell back, revealing a clean-cut channel in the coral. There was no doubt this was the moat of Fort St Andrew.

While Andrew and I measured it up, Vince and Barbara followed the zigzagging ditch. Naturally we were elated at our early success and spent the rest of the day searching the area.

The spoil from the moat had been used to build up ramparts and several bastion positions and a gateway were apparent. The vertical-sided moat was filled with sea water to a depth of approximately three feet for the first twenty yards at its seawards end. It was uniformly cut and approximately four yards wide at water level. The gateway or gap in the rampart was also four yards wide. The ditch went right across the neck of the promontory with an entrance to the sea at one end and a mangrove swamp at the other. Searching the rampart, Barbara discovered glazed potsherds, while Vince found a small cannonball. Gricelio reckoned it was the type fired from a light cannon, which was probably the heaviest weapon the besieging Spaniards could have dragged through the jungle. Inside the fort there were depressions that might have been attempts at wells and, on the seaward side, a battery position for the guns commanded the harbour entrance or sea-gate. Broken pottery littered the ground everywhere.

Later Vince found evidence of the lookout post on the point, but there was no sign of the battery on the mainland side of the sea-gate. Indeed it looked as if successive landslides had widened the harbour entrance. Whilst the search for historical sites went on, Andrew turned his attention to the natural history of the area.

The Scots' first defences were said to be a twenty-five-foot-high rampart across the neck of the isthmus on which the colony stood. In an attempt to discover this, Linda and I cut our way up the steep slippery ridge behind the village. Insects rose in swarms from the bushes whilst underfoot armies of leafcutter ants busied themselves with their perpetual tasks. At last we reached the crest, panting for breath and bathed in sweat.

'You're not an explorer,' gasped Linda. 'You're a ruddy masochist!'

Alas, there was no rampart and although we did find some brickwork in the supposed area, that was one of our failures. Nor did we find the cemetery of the Scots where the Spanish had reported 400 graves. However, we did discover an overgrown airfield, possibly a wartime strip, which would not be too difficult to reopen and could well be useful for future expeditions.

Underwater the real interest was to look for the wrecks of

various ships reported to have sunk in the bay. One was the *Maurepas*, a French merchantman of forty-two guns.

In December 1698 this fine vessel had sought the protection of the Scots from the Spanish fleet and its captain, Duvivier Thomas, enjoyed the isolated colonists' hospitality as he told them the news of the outside world. Whilst the Frenchmen drank and feasted with their new-found friends, rumours circulated that the *Maurepas*'s hold was filled with treasure taken in a raid on the Spanish port of Cartagena.

Meanwhile, the weather deteriorated and the bay was closed by strong winds blowing straight into the sea entrance. It was to be a tragic Christmas Eve.

John Prebble tells the story in his book, which was our guide.

> On the evening of December 23 there was not a sober man among her officers and crew, and most of them were still drunk the next morning when Captain Thomas unaccountably weighed anchor, set his topsails and mainsail and moved toward the sea-gate. Great rollers were coming through it, but by fool's luck his helmsman managed to ride them well until the wind dropped abruptly. The ship swung to leeward and on to the sunken rock.
>
> Pennecuik, who had been watching in astonishment from the *St Andrew*, ordered his longboat away and was rowed across to the *Maurepas*. He took command with a rare decisiveness, calling for more boats and hauling the Frenchmen off the rock. Little serious damage had been done, and when the ship had weathered the point he advised Thomas to drop his bow and stern anchors and wait for a gentler sea. Forty-five minutes later both cables broke, which was what Pennecuik should have foreseen, the ship spun about and back on to the rock, this time tearing a great hole in her hull. She sank slowly, her timbers parting and her mast snapping, but Pennecuik bravely stayed aboard until he had seen Thomas lashed to a raft. He then stripped off his clothes and walked from the deck into the water. 'Naked as I was born, with much ado I swam ashore. The seas broke over me, under each of which I was at least twenty seconds, and indeed two such more had done my business'. He found Thomas along the beach, half-drowned, and ordered him to be hung by the heels until the water had run out of his lungs. Nearly half the crew of the *Maurepas* had been lost, including all her officers with the exception of Thomas and a lieutenant, and the angry survivors would have cut the throats of both had not Pennecuik sent them aboard the *St Andrew*.
>
> There they were to remain for the next two months, and never,

thought the Scots, were men 'more ungrateful, unreasonable, and uneasy'. They had good reason to be. According to Pennecuik there had been 60,000 pieces of eight in gold and silver aboard their ship, and 30,000 more in trading goods, and the thought of this, lying out there in the bay, would plague the greed of the Scots for weeks.

Thus, following the maps in John Prebble's book, Ruth, Dan, Mel and I took air photographs, charts and compass, sailed out in Domitri's leaky dugout and quickly found the reef. The sea heaved gently under a cloudy sky, heavy with rain, as we took our bearings. Sitting in the bow I passed directions to Dan, who directed Domitri's steering. 'Left, left, bit more, steady, now.' Ruth dropped the marker. In fact the Scots might have approved as we were using inflatable whisky advertising bottles as buoys.

When we had completed the designation of the search area, Mel and I flopped into the warm water. Hoping to pick up a fish for supper, I carried a powerful harpoon gun and swam along the surface with only snorkel gear whilst Mel descended to the seabed at the end of his safety line. Shimmering bubbles mushroomed upwards from the aqualung as the diver quartered the area. The spreading coral was alive with small, brightly coloured fish darting in and out. There was nothing unusual to see but I guessed that the *Maurepas* would have gone down behind the reef. So, having checked the shallow water, we now concentrated our search in the depths beyond. Mel kicked his way down the cliff into the gloom; without a breathing set I could only follow him to about five fathoms, but I could see he was now on a flat sandy floor broken only by the occasional rock. Twenty feet beneath me, guided by his wrist compass, he moved slowly back and forth across the area, his gloved hands reaching up to check dark items on the seabed.

'A few shapes that look as if they might be coral-encrusted cannon in the cliff,' said Mel as he surfaced. 'I've got a couple of pictures.' He handed the underwater camera to Ruth and I helped him aboard. It was getting too dark to see and as we had to conserve our limited air supply I decided to call off the search until next day. As yet there was no definite information, so we secured our buoys against the freshening wind and returned to a dinner of avocado hash.

Next day dawned with bright sunshine and a fairly calm sea. We were over the reef by eight o'clock. The green and yellow plastic whisky bottles still bobbed about in the gentle swell as we dropped down into the grey world. Mel was soon on the sand and I noticed he had changed his search pattern. As I watched I could see he was probing something. Indeed there seemed to be a light-coloured shape, a mound stretching out of visibility. We discussed it on the surface.

'It's over one hundred feet long and about fifteen wide,' reported the diving sergeant. 'There are lumps sticking out of it and the sand in the mound is less dense; after I've broken through the surface I can push a harpoon in easily for its entire length.'

Ruth and Dan listened intently as our voices began to show excitement.

'It certainly sounds just like a wreck, probably buried deep in the sand with encrusted spars projecting,' I said.

'Is it light enough for photographs?' asked Ruth, handing Mel the camera.

He nodded, replaced his mouthpiece and sank on to our find.

The billowing mass of silvery air bubbles drifted up from the seabed as, fifty feet below, my companion worked away at the irregular outline of the sand-covered wreck. The rattle of his demand valve was the only sound to disturb this silent world.

Suspended in the clear, warm water, I watched for the diver's signal. Then, for no good reason, I turned round and an awful lump formed instantly in my throat. The shark, its great tail moving rhythmically from side to side, was approaching in slow motion. The pointed head, the beady unblinking eye, the narrow fins, all blended into one blue-green, streamlined shape.

My harpoon gun came up instantly and, as it did, the denizen of the deep swung past; swimming effortlessly he was soon lost beyond the misty limit of the underwater visibility. The theme tune from *Jaws* was still echoing through my mind when, somewhat thankfully, I climbed aboard our boat.

Having checked the position of what we hoped would be the *Maurepas*, we now turned our attention to the next mystery, the site of Acla. Ricardo, a helpful witch-doctor, had told us of ruins on a nearby islet and, visiting the tiny outcrop of coral, we did indeed find pottery and bricks. Gricelio thought it had been a battery position for the defence of the anchorage, probably Spanish, although some of the pottery looked Dutch. Whilst we lunched I spread out the charts and maps of the

Vince and Barbara Martinelli examine the jungle-covered ruins of Fort St Andrews, Caledonia Bay 1976

The Avon Sea-raider on sea trials off Dover 1977. Designed jointly by Royal Engineer Junior Leaders and the Avon Rubber Company, this inflatable gunboat carried a ·30 Browning MG and an 84mm Carl Gustav recoilless anti-tank gun. Capt Russ Tolley RE at the helm

Left: The attack on 'Jaws', Ickham Pond, May 1977

Right: 'I've a feeling I'm being followed'. JB-S, speaking at the launching of Operation Drake in New York in 1978, demonstrates the sort of hazard Young Explorers will have to face

Left: The author teaching a Junior Leader to shoot at Dover

Right: JB-S with potential Young Explorers. Later Nicholas Hopkins (with *matchete*) won a place on Operation Drake awarded by Mr Walter H. Annenberg

The Operation Drake executives at the launching reception at Buckingham Palace on 13 December 1977, the 400th anniversary of Francis Drake's departure from Plymouth.
L to r: Mrs Barbara Martinelli (USA), Miss Ruth Mindel (PR), Mr Andrew Mitchell (zoologist), Maj Bill Kingston (publicity), Cmdr Graham Shaw (RN rep), Mrs F. G. Caldwell (philatelic matters), Mr George Baker (foreign and diplomatic affairs), Gen Sir John Mogg (chairman), Maj-Gen F. G. Caldwell (scientific committee), HRH The Prince of Wales, Mr Frank Taylor (treasurer), Lt-Col John Blashford Snell (director of operations), Mr Otto Roethenmund (Explorers Club, USA), Capt Jim Masters (DAQMG), Mr Mervyn Price (director of administration), Mr Richard Snailham (historian), Mr Maldwin Drummond (ship committee), Mr Freddie Rodger (scientific committee), Mrs Judith Blashford-Snell (co-ordinator UK support organization)

The 150-ton British brigantine *Eye of the Wind*, base ship for Operation Drake

coastline that had been annotated by our friends in Panama City.

'Acla is supposed to lie between these two rivers,' I explained, 'and in fact this river is called the Aglatomate.'

'But they must have had a harbour,' said Vince.

'Yes,' I agreed. 'That's the mystery. There's a cliff, a reef or a mangrove swamp right the way along the coast.'

From the sea we couldn't even identify the two rivers. As we scanned the jungle shoreline with binoculars, the witch-doctor said, 'You want go there?'

'Can you get a boat through that reef, Ricardo?'

'*Si*,' he grunted. '*Es posible*.'

'Come on then, Domitri, let's go,' I ordered.

'This I must film,' remarked Chris, looking at the line of boiling surf.

Approaching the reef, we could see exposed heads of jagged coral projecting from the swirling foam. For a moment it looked dangerous and especially when Domitri's motor stopped momentarily. But then I saw something that was only visible from very close in shore. There was a gap in the reef. In fact it almost overlapped itself and if you knew the way, you could slip safely into a sheltered cove on the far side.

On the palm-fringed beach dozens of Indian dugouts were drawn up whilst the owners harvested the precious coconut in the forest.

'*Señor*,' said Ricardo, 'There is a wall in the jungle, I see it as a boy.' Ricardo was easily sixty so I was not too hopeful that he would actually find something. Nevertheless, we split up, with one party going to the banks of the Aglatomate, whilst the other searched the shore and the Rio Aglaseniqua, the northern river.

Ricardo, Vince and I cut deep into a bamboo thicket which showed signs of flooding, but we found no walls nor any evidence of man. Back on the beach we discovered why the rivers had been invisible from seaward; during the dry season a high sandbar extended right across their mouths. However, it was late in the afternoon and I decided that it all looked like a wild-goose chase.

'Well, Ricardo, we'd better get back,' I said.

'It here somewhere, I know, *señor*,' he grumbled and as we walked to the beach, the old man darted about amongst the trees trying to find his wall.

We were about 200 yards from the boats when I heard the excited chatter of monkeys overhead and paused to watch a troop leaping through the tall palms. Suddenly a black, furry, feline creature, about twice the size of a domestic cat, leapt out of a tree, hurtled across the path and shot up a palm.

'What the . . .' started Vince.

'He eat ze mono,' Ricardo informed us.

'I don't know what it is, we'll have to ask Andrew,' I said, as we looked for further signs of the strange cat-like creature with a foxy face and a bush tail.* Ricardo wasn't interested; he'd met a small Cuna boy with a dog and was jabbering and pointing excitedly. The boy nodded and pointed.

'He knows, *señor*,' grinned the sage.

So we retraced our footsteps and then took a side trail leading deeper into the forest. After only a few dozen paces we were standing in a freshly burnt clearing. The boy pointed his machete at a tumbledown pile of stones running from one side of the clearing to the other. Apparently he had been burning the jungle to make space to plant coconuts, and had found the wall. I felt a surge of excitement as I called out to the rest of the team.

'Over here, over here, we've found something!'

Dan and Linda arrived and, together with Vince, we started measuring the dimensions. It ran on a magnetic bearing of eighty degrees with an average width of eleven feet and a height of about three feet. A bastion appeared to project at right angles; between the wall and the sea Gricelio was already finding pottery and, most important, glass. Lines of stones appeared to mark the foundations of buildings.

'What do you think?' I asked our archaeologist.

'I think you have discovered Acla,' he said solemnly.

Casting around in the surrounding jungle, we found the answer to the problem of the river. In the intervening centuries it had changed course. An earlier bed alongside the wall was just visible. On the shore Dan had located a small quarry and a low rampart, but it would be dark in an hour, so we returned to our base and continued the investigation next day.

Another visit uncovered more artefacts and enabled me to make a sketch map of the area. However, violent squalls were now striking the bay daily and a fair-sized waterspout had

* Andrew later said he thought it was a 'high wood dog', or possibly a type of jaguarondi.

passed five miles to the north. It was 24 April, St George's Day, and I knew the rains were coming.

We rose early on our last day, breakfasted on our US Army rations and loaded the long piraguas. The used pots and pans, plus a pile of surplus rations, we gave to the Cuna girls in whose huts we had stayed.

In the sea-gate a large green sea-turtle lay sentry-like and watched us leave. The palms waved in the breeze above the ruined fort and, looking back, I could easily imagine a lone piper playing a lament on the deserted headland. An hour or so later we landed at Mulatudo. José, an albino, kindly let us stay in his two-storey tin-roofed home and even found some beds and sheets for a few of us.

Next day, we hoped, the aircraft would arrive to take us home. Meanwhile we talked to the Indians and watched the young people dancing. Girls with pudding-basin hairstyles and brightly coloured dresses shook their *maraccas* at dancing boys with pipes of Pan.

'You pay one dollar for every photo,' demanded a grim elder. As I was using a cine camera this would clearly be expensive so we gave him a dollar to cover everyone's pictures!

In the village hall the wizened old chief listened carefully to my account of our work, which was translated from English to Spanish by Gricelio and from Spanish to Cuna by the schoolmaster. The chief did not smile and I believe he was glad the foreigners were leaving, although I did not discover what he had to hide.

By the school we were shown a large cannon barrel, sixty-seven inches long and thirteen inches at the breech.

'*Escoces*,' grunted the schoolmaster, pointing at the gun, but it was too rusty to be sure.

'It come Punta Escoces, one white man bring, many years ago,' continued our guide. 'White man, son of Dr Paterson.'

'That's not possible,' said Dan, 'but how do they know about Paterson?'

'Oh, it's in the folklore, I suppose,' said Chris. I had remembered seeing children with wooden effigies of a man in a top hat and frock coat. Another mystery.

As darkness fell and the humidity seemed to close in on us, little lamps with naked flames flickered in the tightly packed huts. From the assembly hall came an eerie chanting as women bent over their needlework, responding to the exortations of a priest – or was he a politician? The ceremony was beyond our understanding so we retired to the *cantina* to drink a reasonably cool beer and watch a small pet monkey chasing cockroaches.

As I went to bed I saw José by the glow of his cigarette, sitting in a dark corner of his verandah.

'Any mosquitoes?' I inquired.

'No mosquitoes, *señor*,' he replied and, thankful that I needn't unpack my net, I flopped on to the white sheet and the lumpy mattress. As I slipped into unconscious oblivion I felt something prick my toe. Assuming it was an insect I kicked out, then fell asleep.

The storm broke at 1.15 a.m. and the monsoon rain upon the tin roof would have woken the dead. Then I realized my bed was wet.

'Oh, hell,' I thought, 'the rain's coming in.'

As I rose to investigate I felt the call of nature and so, groping for my torch, I stumbled down the external staircase to the evil-smelling loo. The rain had ceased as I ascended again, but my torch revealed something that made me freeze. The stairs were dripping with blood. In six bounds I was in my room and, supposing murder to have been committed, seized my harpoon gun in defence. As I did so something brushed my hair, and, raising my torch beam, I saw a bat flitting around the room. Then the light caught the bed and to my dismay I saw it was drenched in blood which, even now, was dripping on to the floor and forming bright red pools. My legs were scarlet from the knees down.

'Ruth,' I hissed through the cubicle wall.

'What is it?' came a sleepy reply.

'You'd better give me a hand, I think I've cut a vein or something,' I whispered.

Ruth padded in.

'Mind where you tread,' I cautioned.

'What on earth . . .,' she stood looking at me in horror.

Dan arrived next. 'Hell, John,' he said, 'what did you do?'

I could remember nothing untoward happening, except the prick in my toe just before I'd fallen asleep. Having cleaned me up Dan looked puzzled.

'I've never seen anyone bleed so much from such a tiny cut!' exclaimed the doctor. 'It's about a quarter of an inch long on your toe.' Then he added, 'Say, is there any history of blood disease in your family?' On being assured that there wasn't, he asked, 'Have you cut yourself recently?'

'Yes,' I replied, 'yesterday on my knuckle.'

There Dan found a perfect scab. So, dosing me with antibiotics and plastering up the cut, he left me to sleep.

At dawn the room looked like a slaughter-yard and, interestingly, the blood had still not congealed.

'John, I've made some inquiries,' said Dan at breakfast. 'I reckon that bat you saw was a vampire. Apparently the local people are often bitten; and because the creature injects you with a powerful anti-coagulant to make it easier for them to drink your blood, you will bleed profusely,' he explained.

Of course I should have remembered how our horses had suffered during the Darien crossing in 1972. 'There's only a four per cent chance of a bat carrying rabies,' Dan continued, 'but I suggest you start the shots the moment we get back to Panama City.'

Thus in the months that followed I was to undergo no less than three different series of anti-rabies injections, a total of thirty-two jabs in my stomach and backside. By comparison the bite was nothing, so I do hope that the bat got alcohol poisoning from his cup of my blood.

Our plane arrived on time and as we flew back to Panama, the sky grew dark, waterspouts raced across the bay and the rains came, bringing the mosquitoes and the dreaded malaria that had decimated the early settlers.

In a very short time, our team had achieved an incredible amount and world-wide interest followed. We had discovered all the major sites and, of course, a detailed examination must follow. Thus we had prepared the way for a larger-scale expedition. There will be money to raise, a team to recruit and equipment to assemble before all the mysteries of Caledonia Bay can be explored.

But one thing is certain: we all came back with the utmost respect for the brave Scots who died in those steaming jungles almost 300 years before.

11. Adventurous living

'How would you like to command the Junior Leaders Regiment?' asked the brigadier. Inwardly I gasped and my mind flashed back thirteen years to when I had commanded a troop of young sappers at Old Park Barracks, Dover. I remembered the frustrations and the good times, the disappointments and the achievements.

'May I think about it and let you know on Monday, sir?' I replied.

By the time I had reached Thirsk that evening my own mind was made up. The regiment had enormous potential, but because the school-leaving age had been raised to sixteen the Army had felt it necessary to disband this elite unit of boys who previously had joined the corps at fifteen. However, following the rise in the school-leaving age, there had been no decrease in recruiting; indeed the flow had continued unchecked and thus the regiment had remained. Now it was short of equipment, the barracks urgently needed redecoration and there were many other frustrations. It was a challenge!

Over dinner that weekend I filled Judith's glass to the brim and then said, 'I have been offered a new job.'

'I hope it's nearer the girls' school,' replied my tigress, ever anxious about her cubs.

Sipping my wine, I smiled.

'The Junior Leaders Regiment.'

Judith gulped. 'But you hated the place and they all thought you were mad!'

'Well the lads were super; it was just the shortages of everything that annoyed me,' I replied.

'Oh! well,' said she. 'Dover to Blandford can't be worse than the journey from Thirsk – when do we move?'

At Old Park Barracks civilian staff who just remembered me from 1962 prepared to resign!

The aim of the regiment was to train young men as future

non-commissioned officers and warrant officers in the Royal Engineers. Selected boys spent fifteen months with the unit being prepared to join the adult ranks of the corps.

We arrived in May 1976. Napier House, the official quarters, was staffed by two delightful ladies who had looked after many commanding officers. There was also a smart and enthusiastic NCO, Corporal Thomas from South London, as my driver and Mr Capon to keep me spick and span.

My predecessors had fought a long battle to put the unit back into a forward gear and now it was up to me to carry on the movement. I was extremely lucky to have an excellent RSM, WO 1 Mansley, who had been with us on the Blue Nile and Dahlak Quest expeditions. He was a keen member of SES and a man with a great sense of both discipline and humour. There were other old friends, and Jim Grant, Judith's uncle, was a retired officer on the staff. The quartermaster, a vital man, was Lieutenant-Colonel Bob Brown, who had served for thirty-nine years in the corps. John Russell-Jones, my adjutant, was an efficient but humorous officer with a distinct appreciation of girls and parties. I found him very easy to work with!

I have always enjoyed the Army and love being with soldiers, but I realized that, as a lieutenant-colonel in command, this was my last job that would really bring me into close contact with them. It is said that the best appointments in the Royal Engineers are as a commander of a troop and a squadron, but I was determined to enjoy being commanding officer! Nevertheless, I looked back on some very amusing and happy days with my first troop in Cyprus.

I was there in October 1958 during one of those truces for which weakened terrorist organizations often beg and unfortunately politicians sometimes allow in the vain hope of winning political advantage. Sure enough, as soon as they had re-equipped and filled the gaps in their organization, EOKA launched its last big offensive. All over Cyprus ambushes and bombings took place. In an effort to quell one particular region, a battalion of Grenadier Guards was sent into the field. My troop was to support them and thus, on a wet winter's evening, we found ourselves harbouring in broken country. Our sections were quickly deployed to the rifle companies whilst I established my small headquarters near battalion HQ. The first thing and, indeed, one of great importance, was to site the thunderbox.

'Where would you like it, sir?' asked my headquarters corporal.

'That spot by the trees looks well drained, nicely concealed and has a pleasant view,' I replied. So my fine oak portable lavatory was erected under a Karib tree so that, when enthroned at dawn, I might survey the mountains of Turkey some forty miles distant.

The next day the corporal reported that the thunderbox must be moved as it was 'full up'.

'Full up?' I gasped, 'with only five of us here?'

''Fraid so, sir. It's them Guards sergeants using it.'

This was an insult of the highest order. An officer's thunderbox is a very private thing; although I allowed my own soldiers to use it as a special privilege, it was gross insolence for outsiders to intrude. The proximity of the device to the Guards sergeants' mess was clearly too great a temptation. Regretfully I ordered the thunderbox to be moved westward, some sixty paces.

Alas, the next morning it was found to be 'full' again. It really was too much, and I was of a mind to report the matter when my corporal, a devious but ingenious man, suggested an alternative plan to dissuade the trespassers.

'You may recall, sir, we have a hundredweight of home-made explosive that we captured yesterday,' he smirked. 'Might I suggest that we place a minute quantity of this, with a simple booby-trap switch beneath the toilet, to be operated by anyone seating himself thereon?'

The idea appealed to me. 'What about us?' I inquired.

'We shall leave a safety pin on the ground by the switch, sir. All Royal Engineers, before seating, must replace the pin,' replied the corporal.

'Sounds all right,' I said. 'Let's hope none of us is taken short.'

'With Sapper Rampling's cooking, sir, I think the reverse more likely,' assured the NCO.

It was an hour after dark and I was in the battalion operations room taking a turn as duty officer when I heard a dull 'boom'. This was followed by a shout of 'Medical orderly, medical orderly'. The padre came in to relieve me and I asked him what the medic had been called for.

'Oh! one of the sergeants sat on a stove; bit singed, I gather!' replied the vicar.

Hurrying back to our lines, I found my men grouped about the thunderbox – or, I should say, the remains thereof. The hessian screen lay on the ground and the shattered timbers were scattered around the sump. The black plastic seat was fifteen feet away and the roll of soft white paper trailed sadly across the field. The pungent smell of explosive was heavy in the evening air.

'About 2100 hours, sir,' reported the corporal, 'Rampling and I perceived a light bobbing across the field. "Stand to lads," I says, "here comes the enemy." We sees the light go behind the screen and a few seconds later there is the sound of a belt buckle on wood and then, sir, a big bang.'

The wreckage told the rest.

'Then there's t'bloke rolling about in t'smoke,' said Rampling, the cook and troop first aid orderly, in his strong Lancashire accent, continuing the tale. 'He can't get up quick like, cos 'is trousers is round 'is ankles and ee's lost 'is belt.'

'Was he badly hurt?' I asked with genuine concern.

'Well, 'ee was making bit of fuss like, but I think it were just shock,' replied Rampling.

It took all next day to rebuild the thunderbox and it was never the same as the old one. A week later, after a long cordon and search operation, most of the battalion regrouped at the main camp. My sections also came in and, having arrived in the middle of the night, they were not familiar with the layout. Unfortunately one of our sapper lance corporals was discovered on the Grenadiers' commanding officer's thunderbox by the battalion adjutant; a man with whom I had already crossed swords on other matters.

'One of your bloody men is on the colonel's thunderbox,' he screamed at me.

I was tired and considered that there were more important things to worry about at that moment. 'I'm sorry,' I grunted, but the adjutant continued to rave about the incident.

'Oh, for Pete's sake,' I retorted, 'I am always finding Guardsmen on my thunderbox and I have a way of dealing with them.'

The adjutant went puce with astonishment and rage and for a moment I thought he would have a seizure.

'You, you, you have a way of dealing with a Guardsman,' he stammered.

'Yes,' said I. 'We blow them up.'

At this moment the commanding officer came in. The adjutant spun round.

'Colonel, Blashford-Snell has been blowing up Guardsmen,' he blurted out.

'Really?' said the CO, looking mildly interested. 'How?'

I explained what had happened, hoping that I sounded more confident than I felt.

'Hmm,' muttered the senior officer, looking stern. 'Can't have that, can we?'

'Certainly not,' snapped the adjutant with obvious satisfaction.

The colonel poked me with his walking-stick and said slowly, 'Your punishment, young man, is that you must write an article on the event for our regimental magazine.'

In November 1958, following our support to the Grenadiers, I moved on to help a gunner regiment sent out from Britain in the infantry role. Their commander was a great character and insisted that I should run a course on terrorist weapons on the day after our arrival. This training was designed to teach all ranks the techniques employed by EOKA, and one lesson was devoted to home-made bombs. We had with us a quantity of captured potassium chlorate. The class, which consisted of most of the officers and NCOs from regimental headquarters, had gathered around us as I showed them how simple it was to mix the chemicals to produce an explosive.

The lesson was adjourned for lunch and, afterwards, we found that owing to the heat, the chlorate had solidified from a fine white powder into a number of solid lumps. Therefore, returning in the early afternoon, I had to produce sufficient powder to make up a small bomb. Without thought, I picked up a safety-match box and used this to pulverize the lumps. The phosphorous particles on the striker surface at once combined with the powerful oxidizing agent and suddenly I saw a thin wisp of smoke – just in time to hurl the entire box, which contained about twenty pounds of chlorate, behind me. With a great 'whoosh' and a brilliant yellow flame, the powder ignited. I sat down rather heavily, my troop NCOs scattered in all directions and the entire class dived for cover – all, that is, except the colonel.

'Get up, get up, you idiots,' he scolded. 'Don't you know every sapper demonstration begins with a bang? Come on, Blashers, stop fooling around, get on with it.'

My face was blackened, my eyebrows had disappeared and my trousers were full of small holes; however, I attempted to smile and continued the lesson as if the whole thing had been intended.

But now, eighteen years later, I was a commanding officer and was expected to take a more serious and responsible view of life. However, there is no doubt that to get the best out of boys, one has to be young at heart. Having a fair degree of choice over the regiment's instructors, I soon gathered a merry band of high-spirited and enthusiastic colleagues.

Basil Pratt, the ex-Olympic canoeist who had been our padre on the Zaire River, arrived as chaplain. Len Wilson, a fighting-fit parachute engineer, came as a squadron commander, whilst expeditioneers Andrew Mitchell and Christopher Sainsbury arrived as temporary civilian lecturers to fill gaps in our education wing. The unit paymaster, Dan Graham, a giant of a man from Cumbria, who climbed mountains with the same determination and skill as he ran the regiment's financial affairs, kindly took on the job of treasurer of SES. There were also horsemen, yachtsmen, dinghy sailors, hang-glider pilots, divers and sportsmen. With such a gang of extroverts, the quality of the officers' mess parties can be imagined! Our guest nights became infamous and a wide variety of after-dinner games wrought havoc with uniforms, limbs and furniture. One such event was the tray race, in which teams of officers tobogganed downstairs on upturned tables or trays in an effort to get through the revolving doors and reach the rose-bed. We were fortunate that our mess manager and her staff had a sense of humour – although she came near to desperation on one occasion, when surveying the effects of a massive feather-pillow fight.

One of my greatest supporters was Betty Starling, my personal assistant, who turned the illegible scribbles that I jotted down during my long drives with Corporal Thomas into neatly typed letters. Meanwhile John Russell-Jones had been posted and his place taken by a light-hearted but highly efficient yachtsman, Peter Enzer. Peter also had a great taste for adventure so we got on well together and, in spite of a severe economic squeeze on everything from transport to telephones, managed to keep the place running fairly happily.

We were always looking for interesting projects to exercise our young men's engineer skills. One day we were asked to help to solve a problem that was causing concern at the village of Ickham.

It transpired that Mr Alf Leggett, a man of great character who ran a lovely Norman hall as a home for elderly folk, had a lifelong passion for goldfish. After an exciting spell of wartime service as a Royal Navy officer, he had sought more peaceful pursuits in this sleepy Kentish village and was renowned for his success as a breeder of these attractive fish. But one day when Alf inspected his pond, he noted a sudden decrease in its population. Next day a further reduction was apparent. A local angling society was consulted.

'Hmm,' its members said. 'Could be a monster perch, gobbling them up,' and set to with rod and line to catch the cannibal. However, in spite of their valiant efforts, Alf's goldfish continued to disappear. The local policeman was consulted and also the Water Board. Alf, armed with a shotgun, sat in an apple tree, waiting to shoot the swine if it surfaced. But although he fired several times, no writhing monster appeared.

'Might be an eel,' suggested a professor of biochemistry.

'Or a heron,' said a senior police officer. 'Had a nasty case of goldfish nicking in the Midlands once – turned out to be a bloody great heron, ate two hundred a day it did!'

Alf rose early, shotgun in hand, and waited for the predator, but none appeared and now only a handful of goldfish remained. Then someone suggested that it was possible that a lady had emptied a tank of tropical fish into the pond when her young son had gone off to boarding school.

'That must be it, then,' said the regulars in the village pub. 'All these mild winters and hot summers we have been having – whatever it is has grown and now it's thriving on Alf's fish.'

Like wildfire the rumour spread through the leafy lanes of East Kent. 'It's the Russians mucking about with the weather that's done it. If that there monster gets into the waterways of England, God only knows what damage it will do.'

News was scarce and the press, smelling a good story, was quickly on to it. Trade at the village pub increased and once their gullets were suitably dampened, locals were quick to recall forgotten tales of dark doings dating back to Chaucer.

Meanwhile, Alf's former naval chums, reading of his difficulties, began to write in from all over the world. My RSM's uncle lived nearby and told Alf that there was only one thing for it – 'Call in the Royal Engineers!' The RSM did a recce and reported that the willow-surrounded pond was set in a beautiful garden next to some glasshouses.

'A few pounds of plastic underwater would certainly kill anything there,' he said, 'but there is no safe place near enough to the pond from which you can see the demolition on firing.'

'We've got an exercise on next week,' I replied. 'We could use one of the Ferrets,* get it close to the water's edge and fire the demolition electrically from inside the turret.'

Thus it was, the following week, that I set out in my staff car to visit the exercise. As we swept through the manor gates I was mildly surprised to notice a large number of cars. Peter Enzer met me and led us across the beautifully mown lawns. Rounding a hedge we came face to face with a tall man in a deer-stalker hat clutching a shotgun.

'Mr Leggett, I presume?' I said. But before he could answer, we were surrounded by a horde of press men. In fact it was later reported that more members of Fleet Street had come to watch the attack on 'Jaws' (as it was instantly nicknamed) than had greeted President Carter on his recent arrival in Britain. Alf had risen to the occasion and had provided a splendid lunch with lashings of booze to cheer on the newspapermen, and whilst I questioned him about the monster the Junior Sappers got down to the mucky business of laying the explosive on the pond bed. Spencer Eade, the local Army public relations officer, was smiling gleefully as he strode up and down amongst the assembled press.

'Must have every national paper in the country here, John,' he enthused.

Whilst the charges were laid the cameramen jockeyed for the best positions for photographing the explosion. In the process, a TV team crowded on to a small footbridge which, much to the joy of their rivals, collapsed, precipitating the luckless crew into the pond.

I was more than conscious of the proximity of the glasshouses and questioned Staff Sergeant Docherty on the quantity of explosive.

'Only a small charge, Colonel,' he said seriously, and I believed him. Finally all was ready. The Junior Leader who was to fire the demolition climbed into the turret of the armoured car, which had now been drawn up behind the hedge,

* A small armoured car.

its machine-gun pointing menacingly at the muddy waters. I moved back amongst the press and the empty bottles.

'All clear,' came the shout from the sentries and, as the count-down commenced, the cameras were raised. 'Three, two, one, fire.'

The roar of the explosion was barely deadened by the water. Great spouts cascaded high into the sky, much of it drifting down upon us. The only immediate casualty was a duck that happened to be passing overhead and laid an egg in fright, to the amusement of all concerned. A subdued cheer went up and champagne corks popped.

I explained that it was unlikely that we should find anything that day, as any monster lurking therein would almost certainly have sunk into the mud. However, the Press was eager for a picture and was delighted when the odd dead minnow was discovered.

'Well, that should have fixed it,' I said, and we strode away across the lawn for a welcome cup of tea in Alf's kitchen. As we did so we came upon a group of old ladies seated on the lawn.

'Good heavens, Alf, I should think they must have been scared out of their wits,' I said.

'No, stone deaf, all of them,' he winked. But as we passed by one old darling reached out and beckoned.

'Mr Leggett,' she wheezed. 'I think I heard something just then.'

Alf bent down and shouted loudly in her ear. 'Don't worry, dear, it was only an atom bomb they've dropped on London.

The poor lady looked perturbed. 'Oh dear, does that mean I shan't get my paper in the morning?' she asked.

Spencer was on the telephone, looking worried. As he came away I said, 'What's up?'

'Oh well, you can't win them all,' he groaned. 'That was my boss on the line. He has just told me not to promote the story after all, but I had to explain that it was too late, we'd done it. Apparently there is a programme on the telly tonight which is critical of defence expenditure and he thinks that our story may not give quite the right image.'

He was right. The story that was carried by almost every paper in the country and many overseas, and told and re-told on television and radio, was far from serious, but it did show boy soldiers having the time of their lives and recruits flowed in! At least the explosion had gone off as planned, no damage had been done and Alf Leggett was happy. Some people didn't think it especially funny, but a lot did. One extremely important person later asked me how on earth it was that the Army managed to lay on such splendid publicity and went on to inquire why it was that the Navy couldn't do the same! Giles drew two splendid cartoons for the *Daily Express* and the next term we had the biggest intake ever in the regiment.

'Now they've caught their little perch we can get back to our goldfish teas in peace' *Cartoon by Giles in* Daily Express, *13 June 1977*

Whether we got the monster or not was questionable, but later Alf discovered a huge perch, stunned, in a hole in the bank. It had defied all attempts to bring it out; only when an electric fish-attracting device was actually pushed into the monster's lair did it finally emerge. Amazingly it recovered and now lives quietly in a Kentish reservoir – a rather nice end to a fishy story!

Of course, training is so much more interesting if it is fun, and there was no doubt that for the fit and motivated youngster the syllabus at Dover was tremendous. One of the most popular activities was the external leadership which was carried out on the moors and mountains of Britain. We also sent boys on Outward Bound courses – of special interest to me because I had now become a member of the Outward Bound Council. I've always been a great believer in the work of this splendid organization, which is founded very much on the four pillars laid down by Kurt Hahn: physical fitness, self-reliance, rescue and public service, and project work. All this fitted in extremely well with the training of the Junior Leaders.

Meanwhile the SES had continued to develop. The membership had grown steadily and Philip Harrison, an energetic businessman from Dorset, had taken over from Dick Snailham as honorary secretary. Lectures given by members of expeditions were as popular as ever and also a useful source of funds. Dabber and Paddy Davis, who run Associated Speakers, a highly efficient lecture agency, did much to help us organize these, as did Barbara Snell, who has another well-organized agency in the north of England.

The world of expeditioning has no hierarchy, no ranks and few prizes. Most explorers are individualists and strongly resent being co-ordinated by anybody. But expeditions, if they are to be successful, must work as a team which, like a chain, is as strong as its weakest link. And there are risks. In August 1976 the British Vulcan Expedition was decimated by an eruption of Mount Sangay in Ecuador. Adrian Ashby-Smith, who had been with us on the Zaire, and his friend, Ron Mace, were killed; Jan Iwandziuk and Dick Snailham were severely injured. It was a horrific story* and a miracle that anyone survived, but in spite of everything, it was team-work that saved them.

After Zaire, I found myself being asked to join many expedition committees, mainly to help them raise funds. At first I did this gladly and several of the groups with which I was associated made notable success. One young man, of whom I was particularly proud, canoed the whole length of the Mississippi River in aid of cancer research. However, there were others with whom I was not so happy to be involved. Quarrels and squabbles broke out in their organizations and usually these were due to inexperience or lack of leadership. Some of the groups even got as far as fighting it out in the press! The newspapers love a first-class row and did nothing to dissuade aggrieved persons from airing their views. It was very like the nineteenth-century verbal battles between explorers. I do not blame the newspapers. In fact, I have a great many friends in

* Told by Richard Snailham in *Sangay Survived* (Hutchinson, 1978).

Fleet Street, so much so that I have often been accused of showmanship; but I would prefer to be called a salesman. It doesn't matter how ambitious, worth while and well planned your expedition may be; unless you can sell the idea to someone, you are unlikely to get the support to bring it to fruition. I believe the modern expedition leader needs to concentrate on two very important aspects of leadership: communication and inspiration. They are particularly applicable to expeditions.

In order to communicate one must co-operate with the media, and learn to live with the tag of being a showman. However, such was our liaison with the media that I was not altogether surprised to hear that when I was 'kidnapped' for the Thames Television programme, 'This Is your Life', our detractors fancied the whole thing had been rigged! If they could have known the momentary fear that I went through when I found strange people closing in on me and an Irish voice saying in my ear, 'Excuse me one moment, Colonel, we want you', they might have been more sympathetic. As it was, it was only by a miracle that I didn't hit Eamonn Andrews in the face with my briefcase and run. When the truth came out I still felt like running, but was assured that many old friends were in the studio having a tremendous party and therefore I couldn't really walk out on them. The evening was the greatest fun. Nobody burst into tears and everyone drank far too much. It was super to have so many chums present, including Charlie Thompson, a Negro from the Darien Gap who had been lifted out of the jungle and flown across the Atlantic especially for the show.

I doubt that the television company realized what they were taking on when they decided to feature the life of an Army explorer; the high-spirited cast was certainly not easy to control. Perhaps Thames Television learnt something of the strange feelings which bring adventurers and explorers together. I've always felt it is really a fellowship of challenge and curiosity. However, there's also the love of travel to bind us together. So often we do not get the chance to stop, see and learn. I remember once asking an African for his definition of a European and getting this reply: 'Someone in a great hurry, who passes in a cloud of dust.' Then he added, 'When you leave you'll forget us.' However, I've always tried to keep in contact with the people I've met. I remember a Zaire hairdresser who told me that he listened to the BBC World

Service, partly to learn English and partly to learn about other lands because he so badly wanted to travel himself. Imagine a boatload of Africans exploring the upper reaches of the Thames!

I often envy hippies who can afford the time and have the inclination to simply sit around and be with people. I do wish that travellers would be more considerate and let folk get to know them. If only they would do this, tourists could help greatly to break down fears in developing nations. This will be particularly true as the bamboo curtain lifts and as the Chinese masses, who are almost completely ignorant of the outside world, meet more foreigners. Of course, tourism isn't always a good thing – I've seen only too clearly how excessive money can corrupt people – but I've always been a great admirer of the Chinese and believe that their morality and their current control of tourism may do much to alleviate the problems that the dark-glasses-and-camera brigade can bring with them.

In York one evening Bill Kingston and I discussed the epic circumnavigation of the world by Sir Francis Drake in 1577. Now, 400 years later, we were in a very different Elizabethan era. Drake had sailed from Plymouth with five small ships. Many of the crew were underprivileged youngsters from Devon. They'd been told that they were to look for the legendary Southern Continent, *Terra Australis Incognita*, but the real purpose was secret, known only to Queen Elizabeth I and Drake.

Once through the Straits of Magellan, Drake's fleet was scattered by storms and he was left to continue with one ship, the *Golden Hind*. But now his true purpose was revealed – to plunder the Spanish Main to reduce our taxes and open up new trade routes. Thus, in 1580, having circumnavigated the world, he returned laden with treasure, able to give his Queen much-needed wealth, his sponsors a 4000 per cent profit, and the nation new trade routes. In 1580 England had many problems, but Drake's voyage provided the sort of inspiration and leadership to which youth always seem to respond.

Since 1974 many of us in SES had been concerned about the growing demand by youngsters from all over the world for an ambitious project in which they could take part. Thus, a number of explorers in Britain and North America began to plan an adventurous and imaginative expedition which would challenge the young and enable them to help others. We wanted to involve the maximum number from many lands. The members of our planning group led exciting lives and felt that perhaps it was time to put something back in the pot and help others to enjoy the same opportunities. Inspired by the Elizabethan sea voyages, we decided to call this new enterprise Operation Drake, although we could not promise our sponsors a 4000 per cent dividend, any reduction in income tax or greatly increased trading facilities. However, it was our hope that the young people would profit through experience and international understanding and that the tasks carried out would be of real benefit to mankind. If we are to have an eye to the future, I believe we must look to our young people. I had spent a great deal of time talking to youngsters about their hopes and aspirations. It is quite clear that there are just as many, indeed probably more, with the same spirit of adventure as Raleigh, Hawkins and Drake possessed.

The youth of today want to be stretched and challenged. In the past, National Service went some way to do this and more recently other outdoor activities have been offered. There are, however, many young people who do not regard the latter as true challenges with a real sense of purpose behind them. Prince Charles summed it up in a phrase when he said that the youth of today wanted 'some of the challenges of war in a peacetime situation'. None of us wanted war, but we knew that expeditions could offer unrivalled opportunities of this type. However, travel is costly and you often have to produce a return ticket to even get a visa. Frontiers are becoming increasingly difficult to cross and the world's hostile tribes have exchanged their poisoned arrows for surface-to-air missiles! It's not always easy for the young to find a legal, exciting challenge that they can afford. We had always taken youngsters on our large-scale expeditions and they usually did extremely well, subsequently proving themselves to be excellent ambassadors for the expedition as well as for their sponsors.

All these ideals were very fine but before we could do anything we needed the seed money, and for this we were extremely grateful to Mr Walter Annenberg, lately the American ambassador in London, who had the imagination and foresight to back the new scheme.

The mission of Operation Drake was to circumnavigate the world and to involve the maximum number of young people in

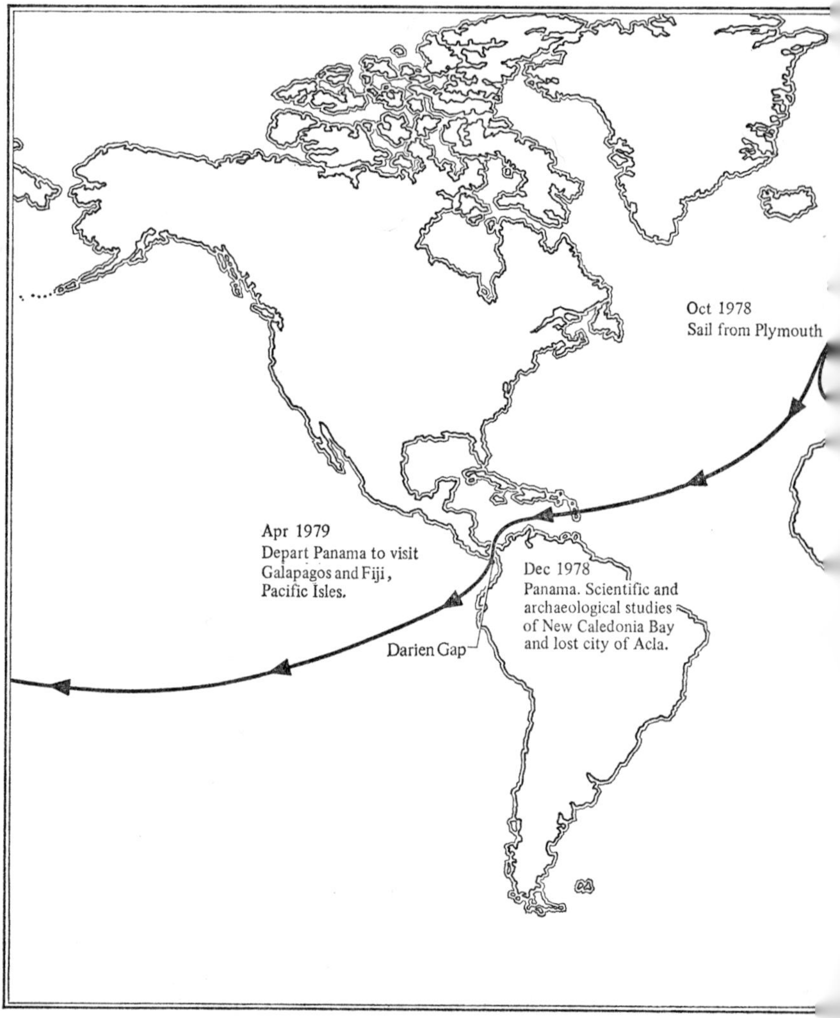

Proposed route of Operation Drake. Marine biological studies will be carried out during the voyage, and in all areas local youngsters and scientists will join the operation

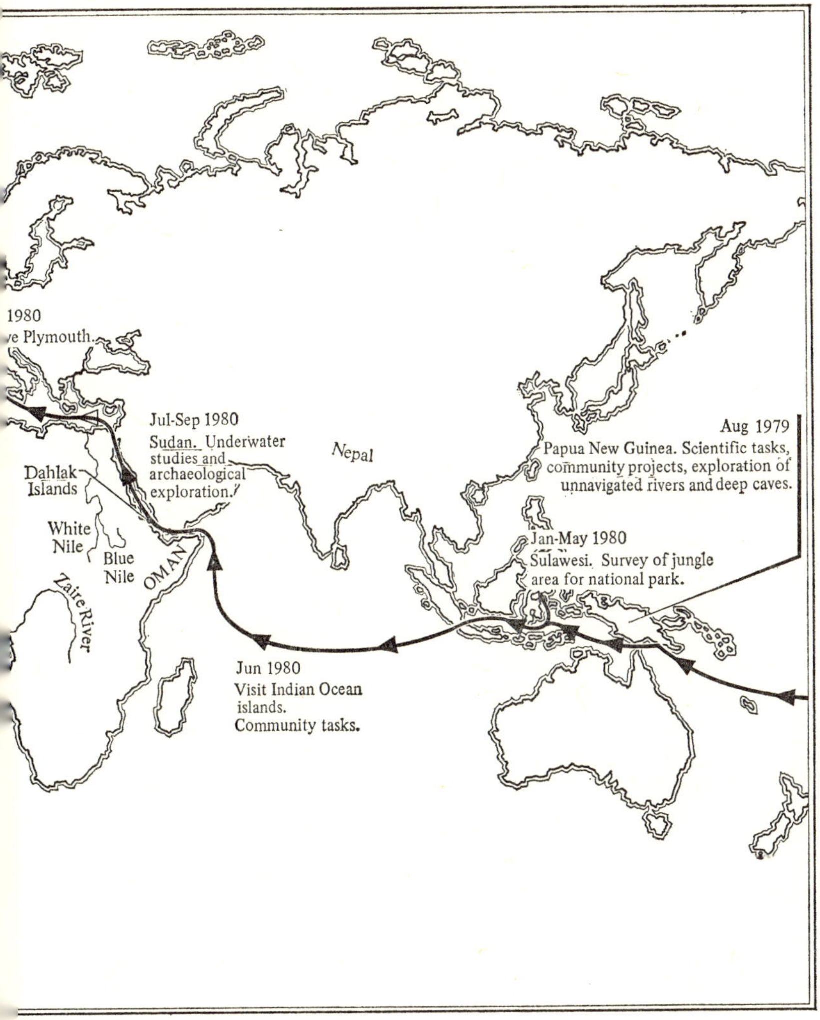

1980
ve Plymouth.
Jul-Sep 1980
Sudan. Underwater studies and archaeological exploration.
Nepal
Aug 1979
Papua New Guinea. Scientific tasks, community projects, exploration of unnavigated rivers and deep caves.
Dahlak Islands
White Nile
Blue Nile
OMAN
Zaire River
Jan-May 1980
Sulawesi. Survey of jungle area for national park.
Jun 1980
Visit Indian Ocean islands.
Community tasks.

challenging but useful community and scientific tasks during the expedition. In October 1978 we planned to sail a 150-ton British brigantine, the *Eye of the Wind*, from Plymouth on a two-year voyage of discovery, during which it would visit various sites for exploration around the world. Carefully selected youngsters, sponsored by companies, charities and individuals, would join the voyage for one of the nine different phases, each approximately three months long. Really challenging tasks of scientific importance and work of assistance to local communities would be carried out in the areas visited before the ship returned to Britain in October 1980. Our route would take us to tropical lands, all of which were approachable by water. We chose these areas specifically; Land-Rovers can cross deserts, hovercraft explore swamps and tractors move in the polar regions, but it is only man on his flat feet, or perhaps an elephant, that can move through jungle with ease. Thus these challenging areas and the undersea regions are the least known and there is certainly plenty of our world left to explore.

Our first expedition would be to Caledonia Bay, after which the two-year-long series of challenging tasks would continue from Panama across the Pacific to Papua New Guinea, where studies of the rain-forests, searches for rare animals and flowers and community aid projects among the developing peoples would be undertaken. Rushing rivers, never before navigated, and dense forest seldom penetrated would be tackled by the young. Similar work would follow in Sulawesi, Indonesia, and the final expedition area was to be in the Red Sea, where we should assist teams of scientists working underwater to investigate the rapid spread of the infamous coral-eating starfish and also carry out important research among the coral reefs. Overall the operation promised to be one of the most exciting and worth-while adventures ever undertaken.

To control the operation we set up a London-based executive committee under the chairmanship of a great outdoorsman, General Sir John Mogg, who had done much to encourage us in establishing SES in the first place and who, until he retired, was the Deputy Supreme Allied Commander, Europe. Also in the team was Ruth Mindel, our resourceful PR lady, who was put in charge of procurement, much to her dismay. An ex-director of Unigate, Mervyn Price, became the vice-chairman in charge of administration, whilst the dynamic Jim Masters, just back from a civilian job in Zaire, took over all personnel and logistic matters. The paperwork was formidable, and what we would have done without Kim Batty and Val Roberts I don't know.

Candidates between the ages of seventeen and twenty-four were to be considered on a world-wide basis. In all a total of 216 young explorers, selected from all walks of life, would be able to travel on the ship. Unlike Drake's crew, we would include girls. It was proposed that scientists would fly to their particular expedition in the field and that the directing staff of the expedition would consist of experienced personnel who would act as group leaders and run the internal organization. During the voyage we should encourage the young explorers to send back film, photographs and reports to their local media and I sincerely hoped that the coverage given would be aimed at them and not at the older hands. I felt that at forty I was getting far too old to inspire a teenager and that someone in their early twenties had a much better chance.

We found the *Eye of the Wind* in Australia and chose it to be our base ship, but we also planned to take with us the giant inflatable raft *David Gestetner*, which was to be used to ferry stores ashore and also as a diving platform.

A detailed scientific programme was prepared in conjunction with the governments concerned. We planned to carry out a series of multi-disciplinary projects and hoped that the data so gained would be of real benefit to the countries. For the young explorers we hoped the programme would create in them a greater awareness of the problems the world has to face.

There was no doubt that Operation Drake was the most ambitious project of its type ever conceived. Equally, the rewards would be high. Young people all over the world would undergo a stimulating experience that should certainly stretch them. When it was over, we felt, they should be able to look back with a sense of achievement on their contribution, both to scientific research and to the communities in the areas they have visited; and, one hopes, they will go on to inspire others.

Throughout the years of planning this massive venture we received the most wonderful encouragement from His Royal Highness The Prince of Wales, himself a great believer in challenge and adventure. Two years previously I had gone to see His Royal Highness at Buckingham Palace and had explained what was in our minds.

As I drove in through the gates Corporal Thomas stopped the staff car at the policeman on duty. 'No bombs in the boot?' grinned the officer. We smiled and drove in. It wasn't until the car had halted in front of the palace that I realized that in the back of the vehicle was an enormous shell which we had picked up that morning from the Ministry of Defence. It was dated about 1823 and was the complete image of the typical anarchist's bomb. Although it was harmless, I could just imagine myself being incarcerated in the Tower if the police had opened the boot.

Prince Charles was clearly enthusiastic about our proposals and graciously said that if we could raise the money, he would consider becoming our patron. Later I was to ask him for some word of encouragement to our potential supporters and he gave me a splendid message which tipped the balance and made the whole thing viable.

As soon as Operation Drake was launched there were final reconnaissances to do and then the organization of selection competitions to pick our young explorers. The response was fantastic and we were swamped with applications. Old friends like Avon, Batchelors, Gestetner's, Package Control and others rallied to our assistance and Operation Drake began to move. However, the story of this great expedition has only just begun.

I am always being asked why on earth we go on doing it. Why is it that this small nation of shopkeepers produces more adventurers and explorers than anywhere else in the world? I don't know the complete answer. But I do remember when we came ashore after making the first descent of the Blue Nile in 1968 that a group of well-wishers had come to the bridge to welcome us in. As our ragged band stepped ashore from our boats a large American lady with a particularly loud voice turned to her husband and said, 'Gee, Elmer, these guys must be crazy.'

'Hush dear,' he said. 'They're British.'

Chronology

1936	Born
1955–7	Sandhurst
1957	Commissioned into Royal Engineers
1958	Joined 33rd Field Squadron RE in Cyprus
1960	Married Judith
1962	Instructor at the Junior Leaders Regiment RE, Dover
1963	Instructor at the Royal Military Academy, Sandhurst
1964	Emma born
1967	Victoria born
1968	The Great Abbai Expedition
1969	The Scientific Exploration Society founded
	The Dahlak Quest Expedition
	Wrote *Weapons and Tactics* (Penguin, 1974)
1970	Ministry of Defence, Whitehall
	Sealed Knot battles
1971	Ministry of Defence
	Sealed Knot battles
1972	British Trans-Americas Expedition
	Squadron Commander, 48th Field Squadron RE, Ripon
1973	With Squadron in Ulster
	Revisit Panama
1974	With Squadron in Oman
	Where the Trails Run Out published (Hutchinson)
1974–5	The Zaire River Expedition
1975	*In the Steps of Stanley* published (Hutchinson)
	Family expedition to Nepal
1976	Caledonia Bay recce expedition
	Commanding officer, the Junior Leaders Regiment RE, Dover
1977	*Expeditions, the Experts' Way* published (Faber)
	Recce in Papua New Guinea
1978	Operation Drake

Index